W9-AHE-274

Karol Wojtyla

John Paul II
A Pope for the People

Text by

LUIGI ACCATTOLI

HEINZ-JOACHIM FISCHER

ARTHUR HERTZBERG

MARCO POLITI

HANSJAKOB STEHLE

Captions by Michael Schrom

Translated from the German by
Russell Stockman

Harry N. Abrams, Inc., Publishers

WAR IS NEVER AN INEVITABLE.
IT IS ALWAYS A DEFEAT FOR MANKIND.

JOHN PAUL II

Contents

Heinz-Joachim Fischer

A PASSIONATE FAITH
A Portrait of John Paul II

The Pope—Mankind's Advocate

Twenty-five years—a quarter century. For this long the world has been watching one man, Karol Wojtyla, Pope John Paul II. He has held his unique office as the head of the Catholic Church for so long that he is the only pope the majority of young people have ever known. As the leader for the millions of "Roman" Christians all over the world. As a spokesman for Christianity on every continent. As perhaps the world's highest moral authority. As that man in the white cassock, who for so long has appeared as reliably as the stars in the heavens on the great stage of St. Peter's in Rome. Karol Wojtyla, the pope.

At one time John Paul II was at the center of the stage and actively dominated the scene. He now appears increasingly frail, bent, and weighted down by all the pomp and ancient protocol that surrounds him. He appears very ill, yet he continues to scrutinize his surroundings with sharp eyes, and to astonish the world with surprising initiatives. He is a pope who involves himself in the great, burning questions of mankind—war and peace, the present and the future, teachings from the past. He speaks convincingly about the lives of individuals, their worth and their dignity, about life and death, with no regard to cultural or religious differences. Life in modern society is too frantic, he admonishes; obsessed with novelty, we race anxiously from one image to the next.

One might have thought that we would have long since grown tired of this particular show with its same lead actor and switched to lighter fare. But it appears that humankind is devoted to this pope.

Over these twenty-five years governments have seen legislatures come and go, a succession of presidents and prime ministers. Party leaders have surfaced, been celebrated, and disappeared again. John Paul II has stayed on. Jesus Christ said, "Go out into all the world," and John Paul II is his emissary. How many fashions have changed in these twenty-five years? How many new products have been invented and discarded again? Perhaps that is precisely why so many people continue to look to this one man.

The pope turned eighty-three in 2003, and now many watch for his appearance at the window of the Apostolic Palace just to reassure themselves that he is still there. When the head of the Church, before thousands in the audience hall at the Vatican, laments "the silence of God" like some Old Testament prophet, it is not only the faithful who are alarmed. When early in 2003 he summoned all his strength to go before representatives of the United Nations—ambassadors of Iraq and the United States among

An alert child but not a happy one. The second son of Karol and Emilia Wojtyla was born on May 18, 1920. A latecomer. His brother, Edmund, was fourteen years older. His sister, Olga, the couple's second child, had died before he was born. His mother was thirty-six at the time of his birth. She gave the child his father's name, Karol. It is said that she never really got over the death of her daughter, and that the gifted, sensitive Karol was "not a happy child."

them—to plead for peace and speak out against war, people everywhere felt deeply moved. When he gropes for words in the oppressive heat at Castel Gandolfo, his summer residence in the Alban Hills, pilgrims sorrow for him.

Whether rich or poor, healthy or infirm, famous or unknown, a believer or not, all feel validated by his essential humanity. And most have a sense that this man is sorely needed—not only as pontifex of the Catholic Church, not only as the representative of Christianity in dialogue with other world religions and cultures, but as a champion of human life.

Karol and Emilia Wojtyla on their wedding day. He was responsible, generous, and indefatigable; she delicate, frail, and passionate. He first served as a non-commissioned officer in the Austro-Hungarian army, then with the rebirth of his homeland after World War I he joined the newly established Polish army, and was stationed as a captain in Wadowice. Karol and Emilia were married for more than two decades, then in 1929 the "always sickly" Emilia died at the age of forty-five.

The Polish Cardinal

On October 16, 1978, in the Vatican's Sistine Chapel, Karol Wojtyla was elected, after eight ballots by 110 cardinals from all over the world. He is the first non-Italian pope in 455 years, the first Slav and Pole in history. Then as now, he hardly seemed a "typical Pole," whatever cliché that might call to mind. To be sure, he adores the Polish language, and expresses himself in it with virtuosity and brilliance as in no other; he himself has affirmed time and again that he is passionately devoted to it. Accordingly, his gift for repartee and unerring wit is best displayed before a Polish audience. He is certainly not "typically" German, or American, or French, or Spanish. But Polish?

The various cardinals of Rome's international Curia betray their origins much more obviously than does their supreme shepherd, unless it is a matter crucial to international politics. In June 1979 John Paul II threw his nationality into the fray when speaking against the Communist regime and on the side of his oppressed compatriots. In a challenge to all the representatives of the state and party leadership he declared: "Permit me, gentlemen, to continue to consider Poland's well-being as my own, and to take a profound interest in it, just as if I were still living in this country and a citizen of this state." As is well known, his statement helped to change world politics.

Above all, Karol Wojtyla was elected in October 1978 because he was a healthy man only fifty-eight years old, who offered the promise of continuity and stability after the mere thirty-three-day reign of the Italian Albino Luciani, John Paul I. The Polish cardinal had formerly served for twenty years in the archbishopric of Kraków, first as suffragan, then as bishopric administrator, and since January 1964 as archbishop. He was named a cardinal in June 1967. This period in his life passed without major incident, and his independent, self-sufficient nature brought him the attention and respect of his superiors only now and again.

The metropolitan of Kraków always stood in the shadow of Poland's primate, Stefan Wyszynski. It was the latter—born in 1901, bishop of Lublin since 1946, archbishop of Gniezno and Warsaw since 1948, named cardinal in 1953—who set the tone for the Polish Church, functioning as a fearless warrior for the faith against the Communist regime and at times the Vatican's all too conciliatory Eastern policy. Accordingly, the Krakówer Wojtyla was always thought of as the second among the princes of the Church in Catholic, Communist Poland. He always let his primate take charge in dealings with the Party and the government, appropriately deferring to him in other matters as well, and Wojtyla appeared to be altogether comfortable in doing so.

Wyszynski accepted this deference as only natural, as the recognition of a hierarchy willed by God. Just how he saw that hierarchy is revealed by an anecdote from the conclave of October 1978. Another cardinal, probably Franz König from Vienna, intimated to the primate that now that John Paul I had died the time might well have come for a Polish pope. Cardinal Wyszynski replied: "But don't you think that at seventy-seven I am too old for such an office?" Only later did it occur to him that the man had in mind the "second" Polish cardinal, by which time he would welcome his subordinate's election with patriotic pride.

Wojtyla the archbishop and cardinal was a versatile, gifted pastor. That was obvious to everyone in Poland. He was unfailingly gracious, though he could become stubborn on occasion if it was a matter of defending the legitimate human interests

ABOVE LEFT

According to a neighbor, Karol's mother repeatedly told her, "You'll see what a great man this little child is going to be." But this was more likely an instance of legend-making after the fact rather than a genuine prophecy.

ABOVE RIGHT

Karol (top left) with his classmates. He was an outstanding goalkeeper. In his report card he received a "very good" in Sports, Singing, Drawing, Religion, and Behavior, a "good" in everything else. One quarter of his elementary school classmates were Jewish, including one of his best friends, Juri Kluger. It is said that Karol frequently volunteered to play on the school's "Jewish" sports team against its "Catholic" one. From childhood, Karol was familiar with Jewish customs. The Wojtyla family remained immune to the latent, widespread anti-Semitism of that time.

of his flock against the Communist authorities, or if he wanted to accomplish something like the construction of a church in Kraków's new housing development of Nowa Huta. During the Second Vatican Council (1962–65), when Catholic bishops from around the world converged on Rome and discovered that they represented a truly global church, the Krakówer was already spoken of as "the one below the primate, though somewhat more flexible." As a cardinal, Karol Wojtyla was by no means unknown, especially among the neighboring German-language church leaders like Franz König in Vienna, Alfred Bengsch in Berlin (also elevated to cardinal in 1967), Joseph Höffner in Cologne, or Joseph Ratzinger in Munich. He won more friends when the Polish bishops visited Germany in the summer of 1978, even though Cardinal Wyszynski led the delegation and received the lion's share of attention. The archbishop of Kraków was accustomed to this and was hardly upset by it. It is possible to become pope even if one is unassuming, and even with German guarantors. But then it becomes infinitely more difficult to remain so.

Karol Wojtyla began to sense as much when on October 16, 1978, on a pleasant autumn afternoon after his election as pope, he stepped out onto the center loggia of St. Peter's before some 200,000 of the faithful and the curious, Catholics and other Christians from all over the world, waiting on Bernini's massive square. It was his first appearance "urbi et orbi"—before the city and the world—as the papal benediction had read for centuries. He still seemed shy, a stranger from a strange land, as he put it. But once he began speaking in Italian, begging forgiveness for his mistakes, and asked for his followers' confidence, he already began to radiate confidence in his new role as "universal bishop," one of the pope's official titles.

Above all, he appeared to be determined to be pope; from the very first days, his decisive words and gestures made that clear. Obviously there was now no doubt but that divine providence had guided him from the remote Polish village of Wadowice, near Kraków, where he was born on May 18, 1920, to the very throne of St. Peter in Rome. If God had taken such pains for a Polish archbishop, he piously reflected, then He must have His reasons.

The delicate boy with a candle in his hand looks a bit like a soldier keeping watch before a shrine. Nineteen twenty-nine, the year this photo was taken, brought Karol two important experiences. The nine-year-old received Holy Communion for the first time, for Christians a symbol and expression of a person's most intimate union with God, and in that same year his mother died. It has often been suggested that Karol Wojtyla's deep devotion to the Virgin somehow relates to that early loss. His father took over for his absent wife. "It often happened," Karol Wojtyla remembers, "that I would wake up in the night and find my father kneeling on the floor." Karol would encounter the image of the praying soldier again in the Bible. "Fasten on the belt of truth; for coat of mail put on integrity; let the shoes on your feet be the gospel of peace, to give you firm footing; and, with all these, take up the great shield of faith" (Ephesians 6:14–16).

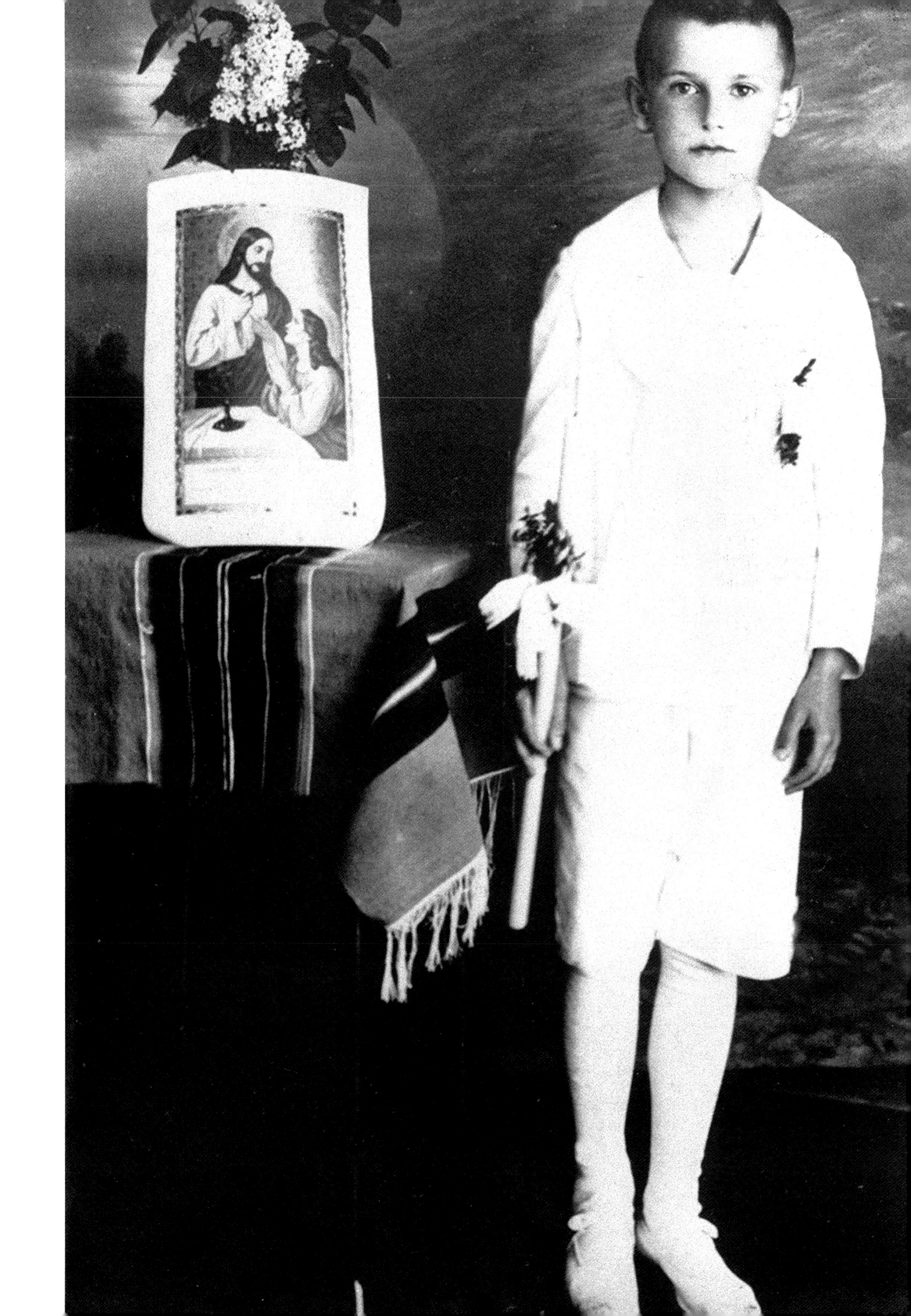

What has followed since the decision of the college of cardinals to select a non-Italian is related, from various points of view, elsewhere in this book. While the pope's activities have been watched by an attentive, often mesmerized public, less attention has been paid to what made Karol Wojtyla from Wadowice the man he is, especially to the story of his childhood and youth. For after the age of fifty-eight a man's personality is unlikely to change significantly, even if he becomes pope. It is fascinating to learn how Karol Wojtyla arrived at his major convictions, how his views of both the world and the faith took shape and solidified, and how the major themes of his pontificate were prefigured in his early years.

Touched by Death—Nurturer of Life

One example of how John Paul II's early life continues to influence him and his pontificate can be found in the long, impassioned debate between the Church leadership in Rome and those who advocate counseling pregnant women about their options. In Germany, for example, one issue is the ability of Catholic counseling centers to participate in the German federal system and offer advice to women in conflict between abortion and continuing their pregnancy. Some wondered why the pope remained so obdurate in his refusal to permit under any circumstances Catholic "certification" permitting abortion with impunity. But those who questioned had not considered the pope's personal history. It turns out that little Karol was what some would call an afterthought, a latecomer born long after his older two siblings. His parents had been married for sixteen years, his mother, Emilia, was a "frail, delicate, and passionate" woman; his father Karol—to quote from his official file from his time as an officer in the Austro-Hungarian army before World War I—"upright, loyal, well-bred, modest, no-nonsense, responsible, generous, and indefatigable."

We know from numerous statements what the pope felt about the notion that at the age of thirty-six his mother, "delicate and always sickly" (and in

As a student, Karol sought the meaning of life with the same earnestness and passion that he attempted to provide later as a priest. Interestingly enough, he did not at first search for answers in the Church, but rather in literature and drama. The philology student loved the works of Rainer Maria Rilke and Fyodor Dostoyevsky. He read Graham Greene and Albert Camus, and himself wrote plays and poems, infused with Polish Romanticism, that were political and patriotic in nature as well as religious. Only later, in the midst of World War II, did he determine to become a priest. In the fall of 1942 he entered Kraków's seminary for the priesthood, which was forbidden by the Nazis but continued to function underground. He began his studies in secret, while remaining true to his love of literature and the theater. Under the German occupation this was not without risk. The stage was often someone's living room or cellar, and the plays were infused with the pathos of an ideal world in accord with the will of God. In 1964, when the Polish primate Cardinal Stefan Wyszynski was asked who the newly appointed archbishop of Kraków might be, he responded succinctly: "A poet." Even as pope, Karol Wojtyla would publish a volume of poems.

1920 dangerously old to consider pregnancy), might have been authorized, after reasonable consultation, to have an abortion. Indeed, in 1974 the Kraków cardinal had established in his archbishopric a fund for single pregnant women—counseling included, needless to say—who chose to keep their child rather than abort. To be sure, the issue is multilayered and complex. Coming from Poland, where there are so many abortions, John Paul II was well aware of this. But pressed again and again by German prelates for a final ruling, he stuck to the Church's moral teachings that he has tirelessly reaffirmed.

His unconditional "yes" to life is also an existential response, this one to Karol Wojtyla's first-hand experience of death. As a child and young man he suffered the brutal intrusion of death into his immediate surroundings, and was deeply moved by the unfathomable *mysterium mortis*, the fact that human life is so constantly at risk and swiftly ended. One of his companions from that time asserts that Karol was not a happy child, in large part because his mother was always sickly and his father eternally worried about her. His mother, herself orphaned at the age of nine and despondent over the early deaths of four of her eight siblings, never wholly recovered from the loss of her second child, her little daughter Olga, early on in her marriage. Emilia died on April 13, 1929, when she was only forty-five. Karol was nine years old at the time, and from then on happiness was beyond his grasp. It was not because of any lack of achievement. His report cards read "very good" after "Religion" and "Behavior," unsurprisingly, but also, less predictably, after "Drawing," "Singing," and "Sports"; he received a "good" after everything else.

At twelve the young Karol had another encounter with death when his twenty-six-year-old brother, Edmund, succumbed to scarlet fever on December 5, 1932. Edmund was a charming, sociable, and athletic young man whom his little brother looked up to and adored more than anyone else. He had studied medicine and had just begun his career as a doctor, in which capacity he became infected by a patient. Karol's pastor, Kazimierz Suder, felt that this additional death in the family was a shock that struck the young boy even harder than the death of his mother. Psychologists would probably judge that a pubescent boy living in the shadow of death is somehow "damaged," or at least "marked," by the experience. To the believing Christian, however, such blows of fate have a meaning. As the inscription on his tombstone reads, and as it was explained to his younger brother, Edmund was "sacrificed to his profession, which placed his young life in the service of mankind." Such sacrifice made sense to Karol, and could be understood as religious renunciation as opposed to blind self-advancement.

When his father died in 1941, Karol Wojtyla finally knew that earthly life could not be counted on, that it could hardly be the highest good, and that he could never recklessly delight in the joys of

“They said to one another, ‘Did we not feel our hearts on fire as he talked with us on the road and explained the scriptures to us?’” (Luke 24:32) This from the gospel, telling of the disciples’ trek with Jesus to Emmaus. One wonders whether the students pictured here also felt themselves to be questioning disciples. One thing is certain: Karol (far right) loved having spiritual discussions while on extended hikes. These young men shared a conviction that politics and religion belong together, that history and salvation are profoundly connected. During the war, in order not to be deported to Germany for forced labor, Karol had to show that he had work in Kraków. In the fall of 1940 he found a job in a chemical factory, first in its quarry, then in the firm’s clarification works. These student years of factory work were both shelter and camouflage. More important, they would help shape his philosophy, and explain his partiality toward working people and unions. “The true greatness of work lies in the person,” he wrote in one of his poems. From this insight he would later develop his scathing criticism of capitalism. His struggles against the exploitation of workers, the unchecked pursuit of profits, and the injustices of today’s world economy have brought him the respect of non-believers, critics of globalization, leftists, and Communists around the world. In the center: Franciszek Macharski, a friend and fellow student whom Wojtyla would name a bishop once he became pope and install as his successor in Kraków.

life and love. Now, as the twenty-one-year-old sadly noted, he was alone, robbed of his next of kin. As it turned out, it was only the Catholic way of life, which he faithfully kept to as a legacy from his own shrinking family and which he could witness all about him in Kraków, that helped him to overcome the fear of death. The birth and development of religious life, impervious to all doubt, with a love for the physical life born out of experience of death—this is the crux of Wojtyla's faith.

The Earthly and the Heavenly Mother

Through death in his family Wojtyla found yet another answer. Affirmation of life is common to all world religions, and important to all deeply religious people. In Christian faith it is firmly rooted in the mystery of death and resurrection, in belief in man's sinfulness—the true *conditio humana*—and his salvation. Wojtyla could only bear the mystery of death already experienced as a child, or bear it better, within the arms of religion, by directing his gaze beyond the earthly toward the hereafter, by meditating on the Christian faith and the familiar rites and consolations of Catholicism. His father was a loving, serious, and rather reserved man who, after the death of his wife, was focused on his little boy. A deeply religious man, he could do nothing else—and nothing better—than to give his son, in addition to his real mother in heaven, the heavenly mother Mary, wholly present in prayer.

It is well known that John Paul II is an ardent devotee of the Virgin and mother of God in general, and especially Poland's Madonna of Częstochowa. He ascribes to that Madonna his survival after the attack on his life on May 13, 1981, when the Turkish assassin Mehmet Ali Agca shot at him during an audience on St. Peter's Square. An "evil force" may have fired the bullets, but a heavenly power steered them away from their fatal target. It would be inappropriate to overinterpret his worship of Mary in psychological terms, and draw from it radical conclusions about his relationship to women. His relationship with the heavenly Madonna may well have bolstered his high esteem for women and led him to keep at a somewhat more respectful distance from them in real life. But more on this later.

No one can dismiss Karol Wojtyla's worship of Mary as mere superstition. To do so would be to foolishly ignore centuries of cultural developments within Christianity, notably artistic achievements.

Sensing God's majesty in the beauty of nature. All his life, Karol Wojtyla has been known for a profound natural mysticism. In 1946 he was ordained and left Poland for two years of additional study in Rome. After his return he qualified as a university lecturer with a study of the German philosopher Max Scheler. Truth, freedom, and personhood are fundamental concepts in his thinking, not unlike that of Martin Buber or Emmanuel Lévinas. But one must not mistake Karol Wojtyla's emphasis on the person for present-day individualism. What interests him is the essence of man. And this—like nature—is part of a divine plan that transcends the individual.

Marian spirituality and theology appealed to him early on and became his very flesh and blood. As recently as the fall of 2002 he urged the reciting of the rosary in honor of the Virgin. His prayer beads had helped Karol Wojtyla surmount his experiences with death, where others might have surrendered to less noble pursuits.

The Polish Madonna made world history on the lapels of the Danzig dockworkers who, as the union Solidarity, defied the Communist regime and its tanks in her image. The Madonna of Fatima, who originated in Portugal in 1917, also plays a major role in twentieth-century Catholic piety, with her mysterious requests and prophecies calling for the "conversion of Russia," to use language of the faithful, or in political terms, the collapse of Communism in Eastern Europe.

The Ideal Family

Karol Wojtyla's time alone with his father—without a mother, his brother, and other close relatives—gave rise to his yearning for an intact family. Though not immune to misfortune, such a traditional family consisting of a father, a mother, and children should at least be safe from human caprice. It is for this reason that John Paul II so frequently refers to Catholic doctrine regarding the loving family and the indissolubility of marriage. It has been the subject of his papal catecheses again and again, both in Rome and on his trips abroad. He never tires of extolling fatherhood and motherhood as a "liberation from the prison of self-interest." His own personal experience of the absence of familial joy is reflected in his idealization of the family. It is evident, for example, when he speaks respectfully but without indulgent understanding of homosexuality, or has the Congregation of the Faith issue statements about it in his name. His is a firm conviction that the family is the bosom and foundation of society. Even more, that the Church's survival as a church for the people requires intact families. Again and again John Paul II has returned to the issues of married love and fidelity, families staying together. As early as November 1981 he proclaimed in an apostolic exhortation—*Familiaris Consortio*—the Church's traditional teachings regarding the family to be an indispensable moral guideline. He would have preferred to elevate such ideals to the status of dogma, so that mankind might finally find the royal road to happiness.

The "Woman Issue"—Love

Through death in the family, Karol Wojtyla the child, the boy, and the student experienced the frailty of human life directly and painfully. One might have thought that such experience would have caused him, a future pope, to wish to become a priest immediately, especially in Catholic Poland, where priests enjoyed an enviable social standing. On graduating at the top of his class, he spoke so impressively—he had already been involved in amateur theater—that Kraków's Archbishop

Sapieha was troubled that such a promising young man did not choose to devote himself to the service of the Church.

But Wojtyla would have none of it, not yet. And not because of girls and the prospect of the celibate life of a Catholic priest. "That was not the problem," John Paul II would write more than half a century later. In his book *Gift and Mystery: On the Fiftieth Anniversary of My Priestly Ordination* we read: "In those years I was gripped above all by a passion for literature, especially dramatic literature, and for the theater. After passing my entrance exams in May 1938 I enrolled at the university [in Kraków] for the course in Polish philology."

Of course, in the thinking of the later celibate, the serenity of age may have toned things down a bit. Considering the pope's effect on people, certainly the female half of mankind, this is a reasonable explanation. Even so, John Paul II was once forced to respond to a cynic somewhat heatedly: "Who told you I committed deadly sins in my youth? That never happened. Can't you believe that a young man can live without mortal sins?" He was referring not to murder and manslaughter, but to the "woman issue."

People naturally wanted to know more. After so many years of priesthood, it is still difficult to imagine how a charming young man in the exciting metropolis of Kraków dealt with the pretty Polish women and with sexuality. But questions about his personal conduct do not reveal much. As a student in 1938 and the following years, Wojtyla would have been removed from the reevaluation of sexual behavior that was taking place, especially among young people, but very close to Catholic Poland with its widespread Catholic morality, its acceptance of the Sixth Commandment upholding marriage and family, its horror of the deadly sin of fornication. John Paul II would later arrive at the concept of "love and responsibility," which as pope he has talked about a great deal.

Wojtyla took his time with his decision to become a priest. As a result, he had plenty of freedom and leisure in which to mature. His career as a student—filled with passion after all, if only for dramatic literature and the theater—lasted more than four years, until the fall of 1942, when he began training for the priesthood. During this extended period in the metropolitan, cultural capital of Kraków, his day-to-day experiences gradually coalesced into a view of man that would stay with him all his life. Perhaps he remained open to the possibility of love, which could have led to marriage. It is idle to speculate about it. Still, it is comforting to think that a future pope did not close himself off from such an important part of life. Perhaps he saw something greater in the Christian notion of renunciation, as extolled by the French writer Paul Claudel in his Catholic drama *Le Soulier de satin* (*The Silken Shoe*; 1919–24). The love between Doña Prouhèze and Don Rodrigo is not a tragic one like Romeo and Juliet's, but one of deliberate renunciation in favor of a mystical, heavenly bond. Having renounced

physical love as a young man, it is likely that the pope has entertained an idealized notion of it all his life.

During this period of youthful turmoil, what the pope has referred to as his "calling" was ripening inside him. He saw himself opting not for marriage, family, and the standard bourgeois life but for something above the trouble and sorrow of this earthly vale of tears. And nothing and no one could talk him out of it. Possibly an even more deciding factor was the most violent storm that suddenly broke out over the young student's Kraków idyll and was one that required wholly different choices.

World War II—The Culture of Death

The six years between 1938 and 1944, during which time Karol Wojtyla graduated from secondary school, studied at university, was admitted to a program of philosophical and theological studies for service in the Church in 1942, and finally entered Archbishop Sapieha's seminar for the priesthood, were a chaotic time—for Kraków, for Poland, and for the world. Events swirling around Wojtyla led the sensitive young man to the view that man is master of neither his own fate nor what takes place around him, that in the mix of good and evil forces it is necessary to put one's trust in something else, a higher power. He could now see death, which he had experienced repeatedly in his own family, occurring on a national scale. "The outbreak of war [on September 1, 1939] altered my course in a rather radical way," the pope has written. This is something of an understatement. A catastrophe had been initiated that would leave nothing unchanged in Kraków or anywhere else the Nazis coveted.

One of the pope's most knowledgeable biographers, the Catholic American writer George Weigel, draws a further conclusion: "I engaged in personal conversations with him [the pope] for hours over the course of a decade. In them I became convinced that the 'passion for mankind' that drives him took shape in him quite early, in the inferno of World War II. There and then he determined to devote his life to defending the dignity and worth of every human life—specifically as a priest in the Catholic Church. There and then he committed himself to helping to create a 'culture of life' as opposed to the many manifestations in late modern times of the 'culture of death'—and he committed himself to doing so not 'in opposition' to modern culture, but by way of an authentic, wholly modern humanism."

Travel is an admitted passion for Karol Wojtyla. It would also become a distinctive feature of his pontificate. He likes taking his own pictures, seeing places for himself. Here he is seen on the Acropolis. He places great religious hopes on Europe, insisting that the war-ravaged continent recall its Christian roots and serve as a model for the rest of the world. After the fall of Communism he, like many others, hoped for a new upsurge of religion, especially among the spiritually starved peoples of Eastern Europe. But his hopes were not fulfilled. His apostolic exhortation *Ecclesia in Europa* is a rather pessimistic assessment of the situation.

The invasion by the German Wehrmacht in September 1939 and the swift conquest of Poland ushered in a frightening time of arrogant German occupation and brutal humiliation of all Poles. It was against the background of the pope's personal experience of war that he made what was to my mind the most powerful demonstration for peace during his pontificate, on February 25, 1981. It was on a cold winter morning in Hiroshima when John Paul II approached the monument to the victims of the atom bomb. He wanted to show the folly of all justifications for the madness of war, to break the senseless and fatal cycle of terror, destruction, and forgetting. He knelt down, and the vision of the pope kneeling silently in front of the Hiroshima memorial served as a powerful symbol for all defenseless people who fear war and pray for peace.

He then stood up and began speaking in Japanese: "War is the work of man. War is the destruction of human life. War is death. To recall Hiroshima means to dedicate yourself to peace. To remember what the inhabitants of this city suffered means to renew one's faith in man, in his ability to do good, in his freedom to choose what is right, in his destiny to turn misfortune into a new beginning." Then, so that people everywhere in an ever smaller and more volatile world might better understand him, he switched into English, French, Spanish, Portuguese, Polish, Chinese, German, and Russian. If ever there were words that went straight to the heart and remained unforgettable, they were the words of this pope who had experienced the pains of racial hatred firsthand, when he shouted in German: "There must never again be war." It was his response as a Christian to the frightening memory of World War II. As pope, however, he would discover that his calls for peace, his entreaties for nonviolent solutions to conflict, fell on deaf ears.

It is astonishing that Karol Wojtyla did not transform his fear of the inhuman, pitiless Nazi occupiers into a general rejection of all things German. As one might expect, as a Pole he harbored contradictory feelings about Germany and the Germans, just as Germans at times have ambivalent feelings about Poland. Countering those negative experiences during the war were ties to German-speaking Central Europe through his father, who had been an official in the Habsburg-Austrian monarchy, as well as his attraction to German culture, evidenced in his intellectual interest in the philosopher Max Scheler (1874–1928).

"Never without my prayer book." No matter where the young man went, he always had with him his breviary. Karol was a sociable fellow and had a large circle of friends, both women and men. But he was also capable of being alone. Solitude became familiar to him early on. When his father died in 1941 the twenty-one-year-old noted sadly, "Now I am all alone." His much-loved brother Edmund, a doctor, had died in 1932, at only twenty-six. The idealization of the family that appears in his later exhortations may have a personal basis. It appears that out of those early sorrows he developed an unshakable faith, a bulwark against the adversities of a world that is only provisional and transitory.

As a priest and bishop, his main ties to the world outside Poland (aside from those to France) ran by way of German-language Catholicism, whether in Vienna or Mainz. The ideas of the German theologians, the openness of many German priests and bishops, and certainly the financial resources of the German Church impressed him. From numerous comments one could almost suspect he could not believe that Germany had also been the home of National Socialism, a hybrid ideology contemptuous of mankind, that such racial hatred and dreams of domination could have originated in a highly cultured Germany in the heart of Christian Europe. He was himself ashamed that Germans had ever descended into such evil and such a perversion of their history.

A Friend of Man

Soberly, without complaint and without accusation, Karol Wojtyla has written about his new life during the war: "To avoid being deported to Germany for forced labor, in the fall of 1940 I began working in a stone quarry that belonged to the Solvay chemical factory." The passionate philology student was forced to become a student-laborer, with all the arduous work that that entailed.

The years in which he was nominally free yet oppressed by war and the occupation were particularly formative. As a student-laborer he reflected a great deal, even wrote poetry. But at twenty he was not one to brood, not filled with grandiose ideas, and by no means a loner fed up with the world and with mankind. On the contrary. Again and again he sought and found contact with people. Never was he in danger of becoming an outsider. In reminiscences of his youth it is astonishing how many people he introduces by name, relating their various fates. He focuses on the positive, commenting, "During the difficult war years I received much good from people." There was the Kydrynski family, which surrounded him "with concern and love"; Jadwiga Lewaj, with whose help he learned French—by far the best of his foreign languages; another woman, Zofia Pozniak, who invited him to concerts in her home. He sought comfort and refuge from the ghastly reality in good-natured intercourse with friends and acquaintances, above all in his passion for acting in a small private theater.

In these reminiscences he does not speak of his work at the quarry and later in the Solvay purification plant as particularly hateful, sweaty labor. He continued to do physical labor for some time, even when he was already studying for the priesthood, and emphasizes that he found "much religious feeling and worldly wisdom" among his fellow workers. It is surely in part thanks to that experience that he is able to ferret such wisdom out of people, draw them out, show their good sides, their special qualities of helpfulness, a sense of justice, sympathy, admiration without envy. Of this period when he was a student-laborer he writes: "Since I was doing manual labor,

I knew very well what physical exertion meant. Every day I was with people who performed the most arduous tasks. I knew their situation, their families, their interests, their humane values, and their dignity. To me personally they were extremely cordial. They knew that I was a student, and they also knew that as soon as circumstances allowed I would take up my studies again. Never did I meet with enmity on that account. I made friends with many of the workers. They would often invite me to their homes. Some of these contacts continue to this day in the form of correspondence." A man who is drawn to people out of passion and conviction never has to complain about being lonely.

The Value of Work—The Dignity of Man

Moved to encapsulate this experience, he wrote: "The whole greatness of work lies in mankind." With this he anticipated—already in 1940—the argument of two encyclicals on human labor. The papal encyclical of September 1981, *Laborem Exercens*, begins with the words: "A man needs to earn his daily bread through work, and only by working can he continually contribute to progress in science and technology as well as to the cultural and moral elevation of society, in community with his brothers and sisters." John Paul II describes the fundamental value and dignity of labor, through which people realize their true selves, through which "human life ought to become more humane." This means that "all activities that have to do with the working process, independent of their objective content, must serve toward the realization of one's humanity, the fulfillment of one's calling as a person." A magnificent idea, which came out of Wojtyla's own experience as a laborer in the quarry near Kraków.

Against All Ideology: Communism—Capitalism—Liberation Theology

Because war was raging and deportation threatened, Karol Wojtyla was forced to work. And because he truly worked hard he saw the world of work realistically, soberly, in human terms, not glorified by ideology. His aversion to all ideologies would stay with him. Thus the encyclical of 1981 teaches that it is inadmissible to erect class conflict between the "world of capital" and the "world of labor." Capital cannot be divorced from labor. The difficulties of working people in the last few decades cannot be solved by the ideologies of liberalism or Marxism, by "collectivizing the means of production" or by "strict capitalism," that is to say by the "unassailable dogma of the exclusive right of private ownership to the means of production." Both capitalist economics, which "considers human labor exclusively in the light of an economic goal" and Marxist materialism (theoretical, practical, or dialectical), which sees "man as the product of economic and production conditions," would deny the "primacy of the person over the object, of human labor over capital." When a quarry worker was fatally wounded in the explosion of a charge of dynamite, Wojtyla burned with a sense of injustice that still moves the churchman whenever man's dignity, his right to a decent life, is violated.

As student-laborer, priest, bishop, cardinal, and pope, Karol Wojtyla measured this against actual socialism, the power structure of Communism within the Soviet bloc, and came to a scathing judgment. Yet when he assumed office in October 1978 there was no indication that as a regime backed by military strength from the Elbe to the Amur and on to Cuba, Communism—a seductive ideology even for many outside its sphere of influence—would ultimately collapse. To the delight of the Kraków archbishop, the Vatican had with great effort managed to slip into the Helsinki Accords in 1975 a few sentences about freedom of conscience and religion. The feeling internationally was that nothing was to disturb the balance between the two great power blocs, not nuclear carelessness, not the Berlin Wall, and certainly not papal pronouncements. John Paul II did not accept that. From the very beginning he tried to stand up for the dignity of man, even against the seemingly overwhelming power of Communism.

Because he was immune to ideology, John Paul II also resisted the "theology of liberation" proclaimed as a new gospel in parts of Latin America and considered in Europe to be the Church's moral obligation. With sure political instinct, on his very first trip in January 1979 to Puebla, Mexico, for the plenary session of the Latin American bishops' conference (CELAM), and also on later visits to Central and South America, he tried to defuse the volatile mixture of politics and Church. John Paul II's influence on developments in Latin America is thus considered of enormous significance in world politics, yet it is frequently upstaged by his successful intervention in formerly Communist-dominated Eastern Europe. The pope's "southern policy" was not so much a fundamental repudiation of the Church's "primary advocacy of the poor" as it was a correction, a clarification in the face of all manner of vague and far-reaching interpretations. It sought to revoke political-

"So many of my contemporaries are losing their lives. Why not me?" Among Karol Wojtyla's early formative experiences were the wholesale killing, the horrifying destruction, and the fanatical racism of World War II. It is unsurprising, then, that in countless speeches he has used the phrase "the culture of death." Also his "never again"—his uncompromising "no" to hatred and war, expulsion, and genocide—derives from his years in Kraków between 1938 and 1944. These years made Karol Wojtyla a political pope, one who is not afraid to point out injustice, unlike his predecessor, Pius XII. It is true that Karol Wojtyla did not join the armed resistance during the war years nor put his life on the line in the cause of the persecuted Jews, but neither did he shut his eyes to what was taking place. Unlike many in his generation, he is by no means one to claim that they had no knowledge of the horror. "Anyone who lived in Poland at that time came into contact with what was happening, if only indirectly. That was my personal experience as well, an experience that I carry with me to this day," he wrote in his book of reminiscences *Gift and Mystery*. His experience would later bear witness to that time most prominently by begging forgiveness for the failures of so many Christians.

Karol Wojtyla on a bicycle tour in the 1950s.

economic experimentation, and above all to depoliticize the clergy. In the cities of Latin America the pope's often-repeated admonition to priests and members of religious orders has been: "You are not political leaders!" From his own personal experience, Karol Wojtyla knew that work is a necessity beyond any ideology, and therefore endeavored to get beyond liberation theology to the truly Christian path.

Accordingly, he never fully understood attacks on the Vatican's corrections of liberation theology, especially by the Congregation of the Faith under Cardinal Ratzinger. To the pope, the whole thrust of Christianity—its advocacy of the poor and the Bible's skepticism toward the rich, the "capitalists," the large landowners, the lords of Latin America's vast *latifundia*—was so obvious that, as he frequently stated in his sermons, he had no need for liberation theology. His astonishing admonition was that the gospel already demanded an eye toward those with too little, in his words, a "primary obligation" to "those who work the soil." That the Church always stood on the side of the rich and powerful, even in Latin America, struck him as an anachronism, and was not part of his Polish experience with Nazis and Communists. Moreover, as head of the Church he saw the dramatic danger of a politicized gospel to the unity of the faithful.

Man Is the Way of the Church

Karol Wojtyla thus turned away from all attempts at self-liberation or self-redemption, no matter how brilliant the analysis of social conditions or what particular scientific findings in developed modern societies they may be based upon. The interests of mankind are not best looked after by man himself, but by God and by his "deputies" on earth. Simple and naive as it is fundamental, this is the view that Karol Wojtyla arrived at during the war years. As pope he has summed it up in the statement, "Man is the way of the Church."

It was only in the fall of 1942, four years after his graduation from secondary school, that he decided to enroll in the department of philosophy and theology at Kraków's Jagiellon University. But he still lived "in the world"—in the home of some of his mother's relatives—not yet behind the sheltering walls of the Church. In addition, under the prevailing terrible circumstances he still had to justify his existence by working as a laborer, for there was the constant threat that he would be deported. In September 1944, when he finally entered the seminary for the priesthood run by the "beloved metropolitan" and later cardinal Adamo Stefano Sapieha, and was able to give up his work in the factory, he began a new life.

Persecuted Jewish Friends—The Golgotha of the Modern World

While Poland was languishing in the choke hold of the German Wehrmacht, while Polish men and women were being humiliated, harassed, beaten, and killed, the student in Kraków also had to witness the Nazis' persecution of the Jews, among them classmates, fellow students, and colleagues from work, as well as his family's Polish landlord back in Wadowice, the doctor who had treated him and introduced him to, as he put it, the "mysteries of the living word." He watched as Gestapo and SS henchmen, the embodiment of evil in human history, strutted about the city streets. Before his own eyes the evil went about its work, disdainful of the worth and dignity of man.

He was well aware that he was being spared the worst, unlike, the pope recalls, the "youngest in our class, who was the first to fall in the war," unlike "my very dear friends, among them several Jews," who fell on the various fronts or died in the concentration camps. One of those camps was no farther from Kraków than his hometown of Wadowice—Auschwitz, the most notorious of them all. This was one more reason for the young theology student to pursue his calling with increased determination, to dedicate himself to doing good for mankind.

His own experience gave him the strength to return to the former concentration camp at Auschwitz while on his first visit to Poland as pope in June 1979. It also gave him the moral authority to call it a "place of horror and racial extermination, built in denial of faith, faith in God and faith in mankind, so as to trample underfoot not only love, but every evidence of human dignity and humanity; a place built on hatred and contempt for man, in the name of an insane ideology."

Then John Paul II became quite personal: "Is it any wonder that the pope who grew up here, who came from the diocese that included the camp at Auschwitz, should have wholly devoted himself to man, to the dignity of man, to the threats to man and his inalienable rights that can be so easily trampled underfoot and eradicated by man? As you know, I have come here many times. Many times I have climbed down into the death cells, many times I have knelt before the wall of death, and I have toured the ruins of the crematoria at Birkenau. I also had to come here as pope. So I have come to kneel down on this Golgotha of our modern world, on these mostly nameless graves. We are standing in a place where we want to think of all races and all people as brothers. If there was bitterness in what I said, I did not say it to accuse anyone. I said it as a reminder. I speak not only thinking of those who died—of four million victims on this vast field—I speak in the name of all whose rights are ignored and violated anywhere in the world. I speak because concern for mankind obligates me, obligates all of us."

But his special thoughts were with that people "whose sons and daughters were condemned to total extermination"—the Jews. This was dramatically apparent: Karol Wojtyla had been personally dismayed, stirred to deepest compassion by the suffering of others. And John Paul II would continue to be profoundly hurt by the Shoah, the murder of millions of Jews. It was for that reason he would become the first pope in history to visit a Jewish house of worship. In April 1986 he prayed in Rome's synagogue with its chief rabbi. And it was for that reason he would admit the guilt of Christians and popes, and humbly state: "The Church deplores all outbreaks of hatred, persecution, and manifestations of anti-Semitism directed against the Jews at any time by anyone, I repeat, by anyone."

Forty years before, he had formed his unshakable convictions in resistance to the horrifying events, the authority, and the spirit of those times. He would later recapitulate: "The final ripening of my calling to the priesthood came during the time of the Second World War, during the Nazi occupation. In view of the widespread evil and the horror of war, the meaning of being a priest and the priest's mission in the world became clearer and clearer." Indeed, it became dangerously clear. Under the occupation of western Poland by the Germans and of eastern Poland by the Soviets according to the terms of the Hitler-Stalin pact, thousands of priests were arrested and deported, some to Dachau, near Munich, the rest to Siberia and to camps in other Soviet republics. How could one's life convictions, one's chosen path, one's fervent faith developed under such conditions ever be shaken? How does one convince a man who has experienced such atrocities in modern times that the human race is making continual progress, that the rule of reason over peoples and nations is immanent, that enlightenment can lead man out of his immature mind-set and allow the good to realize itself? For this pope the "apocalypse" of human self-realization and glory ends in the concentration camp at Auschwitz and the Soviet gulag.

The Churchly Life

Karol Wojtyla determined to place his life as a priest in opposition to such terrors. In a sense, of course, it was no longer his own life but a churchly one. Fortunately, his personality was completely formed, his major life decisions had been made, his basic beliefs established. He now looked to the Church to serve as a kind of mother and father in one. It was to carry out his decisions and solidify his convictions. To his great benefit, the responsible priests and prelates, with the impressive archbishop Sapieha at the forefront, all recognized what a jewel they had in this young man of manifold gifts. He was pious and devout, but no bigot; he was good-looking, but no closet skirt-chaser and no would-be playboy; athletic, but not obtuse; meditative, but no fantast; sociable, but also capable of being alone; active, yet contemplative. He was no egoist, but rather a man who valued other people. Though he could have succeeded in any number of careers, he had

The charisma of Karol Wojtyla did not go unnoticed by Church superiors. At thirty-eight he was named suffragan. In early 1964 he was entrusted with the important and historic see of Kraków, and three years later he was elevated to cardinal. Here we see the new cardinal on his return to Kraków from Rome in 1967.

In the 1960s the Church was infused with a decidedly revolutionary spirit. In 1959, to everyone's astonishment, Pope John XXIII called for an ecumenical council. An event of global importance, it convened in 1962 and continued its deliberations until 1965. For Wojtyla, this was his most influential experience since the war. It brought him in contact with the avant-garde of the Catholic hierarchy gathered together in Rome. The multilingual young bishop breathed deeply of this fresh air suddenly admitted into the Church, and this would have an effect on his home bishopric of Kraków. Political dissidents respected the intellectual archbishop, and saw in the rejuvenated Church, which seemed to be abandoning its courtly traditions and barricaded mentality, a new and up-to-date partner in dialogue. Within the Polish episcopate, Wojtyla was one of the leading voices for reconciliation with the Germans, which took the form of the famous letter from Poland's bishops to their German counterparts in 1965 that concluded with the statement: "We forgive and beg for forgiveness."

set his mind on the priesthood, was committed to it with all his heart, and to all appearances would remain so.

Church authorities were so delighted with the promising theology student that his consecration to the priesthood was moved up, and took place on November 1, 1946. The night of January 18, 1945, the liberation of Kraków by the Red army, had meant only a change in the occupying power. Kraków had fallen out of the frying pan into the fire. Archbishop Sapieha had important plans for the young priest: he was to go to Rome immediately to complete the studies that would qualify him for higher things at home.

And that was how it would be from now on. With all his gifts he had nothing to do but to fulfill the tasks assigned him—no small order. As a guest at the Belgian College in Rome—in this one can see the Church's internationalism even shortly after the war and despite the still bleeding wounds from it—he lived as a student-priest in a building next to the church of San Carlo alle Quattro Fontane in the Via del Quirinale. He studied at the Angelicum, the college of the Dominican Order. It delighted him to be in Rome, a center of world culture and the hub of Catholic Christianity. The Eternal City also opened his eyes to the fact that tradition in continuity offers the best chance for survival in this changeable world.

From Kraków to Rome, Karol Wojtyla was obliged to apply his intelligence and industry, to be friendly in his dealings with fellow students, and to be agreeably respectful to his superiors. Nothing could have been easier. At home they were only waiting for his return to offer him ever-greater undertakings. He acquired his *laurea*, the Roman doctorate in theology, in two years. There was never any need for him to jostle for promotion. The Catholic Church extended to him more opportunities than he could ever make use of, all of them unattainable to the ordinary native of Kraków, up until that day in October 1978 when it learned that it now had a Polish pope.

The two Polish cardinals in the late 1970s: Stefan Wyszynski, the popular, eminently political and combative archbishop of Gniezno and Warsaw since 1948, primate of Poland, and the intellectual, seemingly apolitical Karol Wojtyla. The Polish secret service, which considered Wojtyla a prince of the Church more appealing to the regime, tried in vain to drive a wedge between the two. If Wyszynski was forbidden to leave the country, Wojtyla also stayed home. If a foreign visitor was denied access to the primate, the archbishop of Kraków was also unavailable. Wyszynski championed Karol Wojtyla, yet in some ways they stood at opposite ends of the theological spectrum. Wyszynski tended to view with skepticism the innovations of the Second Vatican Council, and especially the change in Vatican policy toward the East under Pope Paul VI, which now sought fruitful dialogue with the Communist powers.

FOLLOWING SPREADS:

Rome—both the Eternal City and the power center of the Catholic Church. Panoramic view of the city, St. Peter's Square, and the largest church in Christendom.

IN HONORE PRINCIPIS APO
PAVLVS V BVRGHESIVS ROMANVS

Hansjakob Stehle

VISIONS, NOT DIVISIONS

The Pope and Communism

A reformer as pope? John Paul II has had a memorable influence on the world's present political and moral condition, especially the major change in relations between East and West—even if not on the inner workings of his Church. While he was unable to prevent war in Iraq with his call for "courage to fight evil with good" on January 13, 2003, before diplomats from 178 countries, perhaps he helped to prevent something worse. And with a seemingly utopian exhortation twenty-five years earlier he unleashed a revolution. The new pope from Communist-ruled Poland called across the Iron Curtain: "Have no fear! Open your gates, yes, tear them open wide for Christ! Open your national borders, your economic and political systems, your broad areas of culture and of progress to his saving power! Have no fear!"

Who could have imagined back then that such an opening up would ultimately take place in Eastern Europe? In the first year of his pontificate this pope traveled to his Polish homeland—the first pope to visit a Soviet-controlled country—and in Warsaw on June 2, 1979, before more than a million people, including the leaders of the Communist regime, he shouted: "There can be no proper Europe without an independent Poland on its map." The next day he continued, saying, "It is doubtless the will of the Holy Ghost that a Slav as pope should point up the spiritual unity of Christian Europe, this unity of two great traditions: the West and the East."

The spiritual and, for the Communist regime, ideological challenge emanating from this pope was suddenly everywhere: with bold religious zeal and diplomatic shrewdness he forced open doors, behind which stretched a freer, if still uncertain, future. Without Christ there is no true human dignity, he shouted on Warsaw's Victory Square—a sharp affront to the reigning atheists, who nonetheless remained so tame that the pope did not hesitate to call across Poland's borders as well. In Gniezno he meditated on his status as a "Slavic pope," and spoke of his divine calling to lend a voice to the "so often forgotten peoples" of the East, to draw them to the "heart of the Church" and in so doing "make visible the spiritual unity of Christian Europe."

Those were daring words to use while in the middle of the Soviet empire. Then, when upon his departure from Kraków's airport the pope embraced

Karol Wojtyla on his arrival at the conclave in the fall of 1978. Legend has it that there were detailed prophecies that the archbishop of Kraków would be elected. But it was probably Vienna's worldly cardinal Franz König, a man with excellent contacts in the East, who served as "pope maker," steering his colleagues' votes toward the Polish candidate. The year 1978 has gone down in history as the "year of three popes." After the death of the often indecisive and ultimately exhausted Paul VI and the thirty-three-day reign of John Paul I, whom the world remembers as the "smiling pope," the members of the Curia longed for a strong pope in robust health, one who could give new stimulus to the Church. And that is what they got. One of the shortest pontificates in history would be followed by one of the longest.

the Communist head of state Henryk Jablolski—formally but not without warmth—you could almost hear the whispering in the press bleachers. "From this moment on nothing will be same," wrote Mieczyslav Rakovski, journalist and later Poland's last Communist Party leader. Indeed it was evident something had changed, especially when Poland's Solidarity movement, the first free Polish union, survived even the imposition of martial law (1981–83). The enormous influence that issued from Rome, not only on Poland but on all the Communist-ruled countries of Eastern Europe, was summed up in March 1992 by Mikhail Gorbachev after his resignation: "Everything that has happened in Eastern Europe in recent years would have been impossible without the presence of this pope."

Compared to Stalin's dismissive question, "How many *divisions* does the pope have?" this sounded like an overestimation of John Paul II's *visions.* It is true that his call for the removal of East-West barriers and for freedom could be thought of as a kind of declaration of war. But even after 1958, when the thirty-eight-year-old became Poland's youngest bishop as suffragan in Kraków, he was never considered a "cold warrior of the Church" like the Warsaw cardinal and primate Stefan Wyszynski. Recently released documents reveal that even Vadim Pavlov, the representative of the Soviet secret service in Warsaw, reported to Moscow in 1978 that Cardinal Wojtyla, who had been elected pope, while representing "a definite anti-Communist position" and criticizing functionaries of the People's Republic of Poland, "has not openly placed himself against the socialist system." As late as March 2001 the pope forwarded his congratulations on his eighty-fifth birthday to the Russian historian Sirotenko, who in 1945, as a Soviet officer, discovered the seminarist Wojtyla hiding in the Kraków quarry of the Solvay works and saved him from deportation to Siberia by engaging him as an auxiliary translator for the Red Army.

This pontifex has always hoped to build bridges, not tear them down, because—as he said in January 1980—"truth does not permit one to doubt one's opponent," a moral principle that has proved itself in the diplomatic arena as well. John Paul II was determined to continue the Vatican policy that had wrenched concessions for a freer ministry from the Communists in the East, but that was disputed in the West. He disappointed critics of Pope Paul VI's Eastern approach who had expected the Polish pope to dismiss the earlier pontiff's closest as-

"Your Excellency, don't you think it's time for a Polish pope?" It is said that during the conclave Cardinal König put this question to the Polish primate, Cardinal Wyszynski, whereupon the latter—so goes the story—responded: "Don't you think that at seventy-seven I'm too old for such an office?" Only later did he realize that König was campaigning for Poland's "second" cardinal, Karol Wojtyla—by which time he could look up to his former underling with patriotic pride. It is not known which candidate Wojtyla favored, or what he might have been discussing here with his African colleague.

sociate, Agostino Casaroli (1914–1998). But the very opposite occurred: he made Casaroli secretary of state. On June 4, 1979, the pope praised his predecessor's chief diplomat in his Polish homeland before an audience of a hundred thousand amazed believers and introduced Casaroli as the man "who knows the roads to Poland, the roads from Rome to the entire European East" and who "continues to help this great and difficult cause on behalf of the Holy See."

As an emissary of Paul VI, Casaroli had begun to mend severed ties to Eastern Europe in the early 1960s. His travels past the Iron Curtain to Budapest, Prague, Warsaw, Moscow, East Berlin, Bucharest, and Sofia did nothing to shake the Communists' official atheism, but they did create new respect for the pope's Church, long regarded as a "nest of American agents," and more breathing room for its faithful. The pope's native Poland, which had held itself somewhat aloof from the Vatican's Eastern policy at the wish of its primate, Cardinal Stefan Wyszynski, now became the Church's actual proving ground for all of Eastern Europe. With Casaroli's help, John Paul II prepared a sermon that he was to give in early June 1979. With Auschwitz as his pulpit the

One of the Vatican's endless hushed corridors. Much secret diplomacy takes place in these hallways, especially at the time of a papal election. In October 1978 virtually none of the 110 attendant worthies would have bet on Wojtyla, who was chosen on the eighth ballot. This was after the two most promising candidates, the somewhat conservative Genoese cardinal Giuseppe Siri and the venerable Giovanni Benelli, the Vatican's "minister of the interior," had blocked each other, so that neither one could achieve the necessary number of votes.

pope delivered a plea that rose above all national and religious barriers, calling for human rights in "all of Europe, regardless of what faith" and against all those who "force onto people an ideology that subjugates human rights to the requirements of a system." It was an effective move—especially with such a poignant backdrop—both politically and morally.

There was really no need for any mysterious "holy alliance" between the Polish pope and the American secret service, as Watergate whistle-blower Carl Bernstein suspected in 1997. When U.S. president Ronald Reagan met the pope in June 1982, the pope thanked him for information that was by no means news to him, and left no doubt but that he expected the end of Communism in the East through peaceful dialogue and internal collapse rather than in response to the threat of atomic war. To that end, in 1983 and again in 1987 John Paul II made two trips to his homeland, then still governed—shakily—by the martial-law general Wojciech Jaruzelski. In each instance, after a rather cautious start, the pope preached with increasing confidence as a messianic revivalist, and not only in the realm of morals. When he defended "the right of workers to self-government, to independent, autonomous unions" in Gdańsk, a hundred thousand people applauded, including from the front row Lech Walesa, who would soon become the country's first non-Communist head of state.

Perhaps most difficult for the pope's pastoral policy—especially because he was Polish—were the roads (and detours) leading to a politically reformed Orthodox Russia. To be sure, the Soviet representative at the post-Helsinki conference in February 1988 had assured the Vatican's representative that "Lenin's standards for the state's treatment of churches were outdated," and that freedom of conscience was guaranteed by law in the Soviet Union. Still, papal diplomacy was necessary to overcome centuries-old obstacles.

In 1988, when Gorbachev's reforms began to have an effect even on church policy, and the Orthodox Church was permitted to celebrate the thousand-year jubilee of the Christianization of Russia and Ukraine, an ancient antagonism suddenly resurfaced. It dated back to the year 1596, when under pressure from Poland Orthodox Ukrainians subordinated themselves to the pope in Rome in an official "union," but were permitted to continue practicing their own Eastern rite. When the Ukrainians fell under Soviet rule after World War II, Stalin, together with the patriarch of Moscow, had forcibly subjugated this "united" church once again to the Russian Orthodox Church and drove its clergy underground or into emigration. The Ukrainian prelate Cardinal Josif Slipyi, who had lived in the Vatican since 1963, called upon the new pope in 1978 to have nothing to do with Moscow, the "common enemy" of Poles and Ukrainians, and by no means to conclude any pacts with it.

In a difficult balancing act, John Paul II now sought to defend Ukrainians' religious freedom and at the same time further crucial ecumenical dialogue with Russian Orthodoxy. In a letter of March 1979 he appealed to Cardinal Slipyi's "ecumenical spirit"—but in vain. Slipyi's successor, Myroslav Lubachivsky, who also lived in exile in Rome, was a longtime opponent of the pope's ecumenical efforts as well. As late as 1985 Lubachivsky had denied the right of the patriarch of Moscow "to cite the religious significance of Russia's baptism a thousand years ago." That jubilee was in fact Ukraine's, he insisted; the Russians were Mongols, and it was he, Lubachivsky, who deserved the title of patriarch.

His claim and his irreconcilable behavior must have been especially troublesome for a Polish pope, thanks to whose diplomacy Lubachivsky was ultimately permitted to return from his Roman exile to Lwów, in Ukraine, as a cardinal. In November 1987 John Paul II was able to persuade him to relent, and to sign a conciliatory jubilee message from the "united churches" that read: "In the spirit of Christ we extend our hand of forgiveness, reconciliation, and love to the Russian people and the patriarchate of Moscow."

This made it easier for the pope to take up the touchy subject of the jubilee on January 25, 1988, in a letter to the Orthodox Russians, and to rise above what he termed the "centuries-old misunderstandings." A "gradual return to harmony" could be "only positive, especially today, for Orthodox and Catholic successors to the baptism of Kiev," and for the process of a relaxation "in social matters" (*in re civili*), which "raises great hopes" in all who work toward peaceful coexistence. To this allusion to perestroika, already beginning to be felt, the pope linked a call for the unification of Europe, whose Western and Eastern forms of culture belonged together "like the two lungs of a single organism."

Both Eastern and Western observers were startled when scarcely three weeks later, in the encyclical *Sollicitudo Rei Socialis*, the pope distanced himself as much from "liberalistic capitalism in the West" as from "Marxist collectivism in the East," and recommended overcoming their common "tendency toward imperialism" through human solidarity.

These statements made it possible for the pope's secretary of state Casaroli to take in the Orthodox millennial celebration in Moscow, even

Stalin once asked contemptuously, "How many divisions does the Pope have?" But just how strong are the world's strongmen, and how weak the humble servants of God? Soon after John Paul II was inaugurated, the Communist dictators of Eastern Europe felt themselves threatened. Not by his divisions—here a glimpse of the Swiss Guard, the papal bodyguards—but by his visions. The new pope took to the public stage like no pope before him, and missed no opportunity to campaign for human rights and condemn every affront to human dignity. One of Communism's basic tenets is that reality shapes one's consciousness. But consciousness also shapes reality, and the pope's visions electrified the consciousness of the masses.

though the presence of John Paul II himself was not desired. The diplomatic speech with which Casaroli caused his Soviet listeners to prick up their ears during the festivities in the Bolshoi Theater on June 10, 1988, had been written with his boss in the Vatican. For believers, he said, there was a "certain Jesus"—as the gospel once refers to him—the Light of the World, but "it is natural that those who do not share the view of faith judge the fact of Christendom differently, for it stands in very sharp contrast to one of the typical assumptions of modern man, namely... that reason removes mystery from the human horizon as the sun does the shade. Nevertheless, the fact of religion, especially Christendom, continues to be an indisputable reality. It inevitably forces itself onto the attention of the historian, and cannot be ignored by anyone who bears the responsibility of dealing with the reality of people's day-to-day life and their future prospects. The realism of the statesman requires it. And respect for mankind demands it."

This speech by the papal emissary banished the ideology of state atheism to an outmoded past by comparing it to the medieval practice whereby a ruler determined the religious affiliation of his subjects (*Cuius regio eius religio*). From that state of affairs the modern world has increasingly moved away, to the point where now a Christian jubilee may be celebrated "in the society that emerged from the October Revolution of 1917." This, the Vatican believed, allowed one to hope for a "new breath" in Soviet dealings with religion.

Casaroli had something else in his briefcase—something that expressed this message even more plainly: a secret letter from the pope to Gorbachev. In this private letter that Casaroli was able to deliver to "His Excellency Mr. Mikhail Gorbachev" in the Kremlin shortly before his departure on June 13, 1988 (only published by the papal biographer George Weigel in 1999), the pope praised the Soviet-American rapprochement, "especially in view of disarmament," and encouraged the Russian leader to liberalize his religious policy still further, with "confidence that Cardinal Casaroli's visit will open up new perspectives for the condition of Catholics in the Soviet Union."

In that summer of 1988 everything still seemed uncertain. Yet for the pope,

"Vatican City, October 16. The world's 724 million Catholics once again have a new leader. Eighteen days after the unexpected death of Pope John Paul I and ten weeks after the end of the pontificate of Paul VI, the College of Cardinals, in the second conclave of this year, has elected as pope the archbishop of Kraków, Cardinal Karol Wojtyla. He wishes to take the name John Paul II. The 110 cardinals' decision for Wojtyla came in the conclave's eighth ballot, on Monday evening, October 16, the feast of St. Hedwig, patron saint of Silesia. At 6:18 white smoke rose from the chimney above the Sistine chapel. By the time the smoke signal came, some 50,000 people had gathered in St. Peter's Square. At the news that a pope had been chosen, additional thousands streamed toward the square and broke out in excited jubilation. At 6:43 the highest-ranking cardinal, Pericle Felici, announced the name of the new pope."

(FROM AN ANNOUNCEMENT BY THE VATICAN INFORMATION SERVICE, 1978)

a fresh breeze was just now more important than a tempest. The historic turning that John Paul II exploited came faster than a change in Soviet policy in relation to the church; in scarcely two years the pope was able to fill all the vacant sees in Eastern Europe—from Belarus to Siberia, from Lithuania to Bulgaria. Mikhail Gorbachev responded to the pope's private letter only in late August 1989, some fourteen months later: "We are opening ourselves to the world, and are convinced that mutual relaxations are creating a new climate." He announced that he soon wanted to visit his powerful "colleague" in the Vatican. On December 1, 1989, in a "magical moment in history," according to Vatican Radio, Gorbachev was received by the pope in a private audience in Rome. The two talked alone for an hour and a half (the monsignori of the Curia, quietly annoyed, impatiently watched the clock), then a smiling Gorbachev introduced John Paul II to his wife Raïsa: "He's a Slav just like us!"

Because of this, the meeting was hardly the "apocalyptic event" that many critics, notably the ultraconservative bishop Marcel Lefebvre, proclaimed it to be. Meetings between the Vatican and the Kremlin were not the result of black magic, nor did they lead to catastrophic results. At a gathering with diplomats in January 1990, John Paul II explained that the thirst for freedom that was causing walls to fall—physically as well as psychologically—was but the "patient sowing" of "the Vatican's Eastern policy bearing fruit." The pope also emphasized, however, that Vatican diplomacy was always mindful of its pastoral mission, and served "no political ends."

None? The word "politics" has always been problematic for John Paul II. His Church is a global one, and it derives its mission not from this world but from a desire to work in it. The policy pursued by the Vatican made sense only so far as it seemed in the realm of possibility, and the Vatican always had to remain mindful to avoid "expecting the impossible." As papal secretary of state Casaroli said in 1964 after he succeeded in making a first modest agreement with the Communist regime in Hungary, "Even Communists are people, and people change." Twenty-four years later he was able to sign a pact in Budapest that swept nearly all differences off the table.

In the spring of 1990 the pope first entered "post-Communist" territory on a brief trip to Czechoslovakia. As though already anticipating the country's imminent division, he invoked the unity of a "Christian Europe," and warned of the dangers of contamination, of practical materialism and religious indifference: "Outward freedom without inner liberation only produces chaos." He also sought to counter the same danger on his fourth trip as pontiff to Poland, which was now free but many feared losing its national religious harmony. John Paul II appeared not as a "crusader pope brandishing his fist," as the theologian Hans Küng felt at the time, but as a troubled one, vacillating between joy over the turn toward democracy and fear of its price. Even pluralistic states could not do without moral standards in legislation and in public life, he preached. He made his position particularly clear in a speech to the Warsaw diplomatic corps on June 8, 1991: "Along with basic values like the ideological neutrality of the state, human dignity, the priority of the individual over society, and respect for democratic legal standards, one must also develop today, East and West, a vision of Europe as a spiritual-material whole in which prejudice and historic fears, excessive nationalism, and intolerance have been overcome."

The path of this itinerant preacher, increasingly weak physically but spiritually and intellectually unflagging, never blindly points in only a single direction. It often appears as though the secret of his charisma, from which even his critics can never wholly escape, lies in the fact that he can be classified as both a "rightist" and a "leftist"—or neither one nor the other. He was dogmatic about warning South American prophets of a "liberation theology" with Marxist overtones, but at the same time said: "I too am a liberation theologist!" And what he meant by that he explained in his social encyclical of May 1, 1991: "We have seen that it is unacceptable to say that the defeat of so-called Real Socialism leaves capitalism as the only model of economic organization.... The crisis of Marxism does not do away with instances of injustice and suppression in the world...."

John Paul II expressed this sentiment more strongly in June 1991 on that fourth trip to his homeland, now freed from Communism, where one-quarter of the population lived below poverty level. He was preaching in Bialystok on the commandment "Thou shalt not steal," and suddenly his written text struck him as too dry, too staid, and he blurted out what was really on his mind. He rejected both Communist socialism and capitalism: people in the East had been told that private ownership was theft, that the means of production must be entrusted to the collective—in practice to the state and the Party—and now it turned out that private ownership was not theft after all. People had to rethink what was not only a technical problem but a moral one as well. Then the pope's voice nearly broke as he cried out: "Man does not live only for himself, but to enrich society! And the state must protect that! The commandment 'Thou shalt not steal' also means 'Thou shalt not abuse the power of disposing over what you own'—that is to say in such a way that others are thrust into misery! And so we say to the wealthy capitalist societies in the West: Who bears the responsibility for the Third World? Why is it a third world? Look around you! Review your free-market system, this system of private ownership, of private production!"

What the Polish pope was demanding with seemingly socialistic slogans was not in the prepared manuscript of his Bialystok sermon; it was also practically ignored by the media—especially since he himself apologized for diverging from his text. In fact what he said he had already stated, using other words, in his social encyclical *Centesimus Annus* of 1991: The form of exploitation described by Marx has been dealt with in Western societies, but "the estrangement in various forms of exploitation, when men use each other as instruments, has not been overcome."

It seemed almost unbelievable to many freshly converted ex-Communists or old anti-Communists when, in Riga, the capital of the former Republic of Latvia, now out from under Russian rule, the pope preached in September 1993: "The exploitation to which an inhuman capitalism subjected the proletariat was an evil condemned by the social teachings of the Church. And this was basically the grain of truth in Marxism" (*"l'anima di verità"* in the original Italian). Nearly a decade later, in mid-August 2002, when Pope John Paul II once again visited his homeland and was cheered by millions of his compatriots, he called upon them to exhibit greater charity and to uphold the truth "in the face of propaganda that loudly champions the liberalism—a freedom without truth and responsibility—that is increasingly widespread even in our country."

Is Karol Wojtyla then essentially "an economic Communist on the papal throne"? The Viennese economics professor Erich W. Streissler, a Catholic and member of the Order of Knights of the Holy Sepulchre, maintained this in all seriousness in December 2002. A decade earlier he had proposed during a scholarly symposium that the pope's understanding of economy is "distorted by his associates with their vulgar Marxist thinking." This is evident, Streissler insisted, from his first social encyclical, *Laborem Exercens* of 1981, in which the pope promulgates one of the principles of "class warfare," the priority of labor over capital.

In fact, what John Paul II had emphasized in his encyclical was that it is precisely the priority of the individual over the thing that helps to overcome the conflict between capital and labor (or class-warfare motives) in a just, working system. To be sure, this pope has never made it easy for himself—or for his critics and admirers, for that matter—regarding the issue of socialism versus capitalism. For him they have never been mere political or academic concepts. Since they served Poland's Communist Party as ideological slogans to justify its rule, Karol Wojtyla was forced to deal with them even as a young theologian, priest, and professor, and later as bishop of Kraków, not in a polemic way, like many of his fellow clergy, but mainly in terms of a philosophy that conformed to his religious thinking more than the policies of the Church.

In 1958, shortly before he was named suffragan in Kraków, the thirty-eight-year-old theologian and teacher took on the Marxist concept of class struggle in an essay that the regime's censors allowed to be published. Under the title "Justice and Love," he first established that "the materialistic foundations of Marxism are unquestionably permeated with the idea of justice." Wojtyla thus acknowledges the

Triumph. Karol Wojtyla visiting his Polish homeland for the first time as pope in 1979.

struggle of the socially disadvantaged: "One can say without exaggeration that Jesus Christ himself led such a struggle—indeed to a greater extent than those who see in him only the 'first socialist' assume." It is not only a struggle between classes, Wojtyla wrote, but a struggle of peoples, nations, and every individual human being for justice. He pointed out the difficulty that only one of the opposing sides can be right, and that therefore every struggle brings with it devastation, because "the morally good and evil are forever intermixed."

The professor who would become pope twenty years later was realistic in his judgments. His deduction that one must try to set the struggle aside without sacrificing justice was easy enough to formulate theoretically, but if he had drawn from it practical political conclusions they would have been deleted by the Communist censors. Perhaps it was for this reason that he remained more in the realm of the abstract in his principal philosophical work, which appeared in 1969 under the title *The Acting Person.* In that book the world's opposing philosophies were identified as "individualism" and "collectivism," and were traced back to a common root: a non-Christian view of man that does not allow him to participate with others in the community by his own choosing. For Wojtyla the philosopher, the key word for true community was "solidarity." And it would become the slogan with which, as pope, he initiated the beginning of the end of so-called Real Socialism.

Even though he began to work ever more passionately for a Europe whose Christian roots are not to be denied in any future united constitution—his papal call for "reevangelization" seemed both a distress call and a marching order. John Paul II tried to draw up the pastoral political program of such a mission with a European synod in 1999, but apparently he found its results so unsatisfactory that he continued to reflect on the subject—as intellectually vital as ever

PREVIOUS PAGE

Can a mystic change into a politician? Poland, 1979. Millions fill the streets, streaming toward the square where the pope celebrates mass. The red flags have vanished, and there are crosses everywhere. In its coverage of the tour, the German newsmagazine *Der Spiegel* had to ask: "Where are the Communists?" John Paul II swept through his homeland like a monarch. In waves of sound, the crowds greeted him with an old Polish hymn that suddenly seemed like a challenge: "We want God, we want God. We want God in the family, we want God in the books, in the school, we want God in the laws, we want God, we want God...." The union Solidarity came into being. And in his inimitable way John Paul II managed to link the story of salvation to secular history without appearing to be a political messiah. "Is it not the will of the Holy Ghost that this Polish pope, this Slavic pope, should at this very time make visible the spiritual unity of Christian Europe?... Perhaps God chose him so that he might bring to the community of the Church an understanding for words and languages that still sound foreign to ears accustomed to German, Anglo-Saxon, and French sounds."

FOLLOWING SPREAD

In his speeches during his Polish visit the pope used the word "solidarity" with striking frequency—and each time it was met with thunderous applause.

despite his physical infirmity—and almost four years later, in June 2003, signed the hundred-page "post-synodal" exhortation *Ecclesia in Europa*. The document is a dramatic diagnosis that again and again breaks through the clerical style of the Curia and that could even inspire nonbelievers to reflect on the meaning of a secularized society: "The age we are living in, with its own particular challenges, can seem to be a time of bewilderment. Many men and women seem disoriented, uncertain, without hope, and not a few Christians share these feelings.... The loss of Europe's Christian memory and heritage [is] accompanied by a kind of practical agnosticism and religious indifference whereby many Europeans give the impression of living without spiritual roots and somewhat like heirs who have squandered a patrimony entrusted to them by history." The pope therefore recommends a return to Europe's Christian roots, which encourage the priority of law over force, and respect for the rights of individuals and nations. But he also reminds us, as none of his predecessors ever had, of the contributions of other cultures to the Christian European tradition—Roman, Greek, Germanic, Slavic, Jewish, and Muslim. To counter the "deep crisis in values" in present-day Europe, he does not recommend a return to the "confessional state," but rather a Christian "humanization of society."

Fifteen years before, in October 1988, Pope John Paul II had tackled this issue so critically in his speech to the European Parliament in Strasbourg that he caused a certain consternation in conservative Church circles, but critics of the Church were hesitantly admiring. "In our European history," he said, "the line between what is the emperor's and what is God's has been overstepped in both directions. Latin medieval Christianity never escaped the integralist temptation to shut out of the Western community those who did not confess to the true faith. Religious integralism—still practiced today in other parts of the world—seems incompatible with the essential spirit of Europe as molded by the message of Christianity. In our time, conversely, the most terrible threats have come from ideologues who treated society as such or a ruling group as absolutes.... No social system will ever be able to create the kingdom of God on earth!"

Still without pretension and showing no inclination to retire even in the twenty-fifth year of his pontificate and the ninth decade of his life, this pope remains obsessed with his vision of a renewed, peaceful, and Christian Europe.

On January 13, 2003, in a speech to diplomats to the Vatican, he warned against war in Iraq—unsuccessfully—but was able to point to present-day Europe as a successful example of a peaceful solution: "It managed to tear down walls by which it was deformed," and its two-thousand-year-old Christian values should for that reason be anchored in the constitution of the European Union.

On May 2 the pontiff spoke before the papal Social Academy on the dangers of globalization,

REGION
POMORZA

OJCZYZNA

which only aggravates poverty and suffering, and could lead to "exaggerated nationalism, religious fanaticism, and even acts of terror."

On May 3, at the beginning of a trip to Spain, he called on young people "to realize a great dream, the birth of the new Europe of the spirit…not closed in, but open to dialogue."

On June 12, after his hundredth trip abroad, which took him for three days to Croatia, he said he felt like a "wandering missionary" hoping to proclaim salvation to every continent.

On June 22, in Serbia, he preached on reconciliation between peoples, and begged forgiveness for "sins that have been committed by the Catholic Church against mankind, his dignity and his freedom."

On July 5, in view of "the lamentable situation of underdevelopment," he encouraged all Christians to "work toward the humanization of the world."

On August 17, at Castel Gandolfo, his summer residence, the pope warned pilgrims from many countries: "Europe is presently experiencing a crisis of values. The expansion of the European Union by several countries cannot be only a geographical and economic matter, but must translate into a renewed unity of the values of justice and human life."

On September 5 he wrote for the International Prayer for Peace meeting in Aachen a call for dialogue in the lives of nations poisoned by conflict and misery. "We will not accept that war should dominate life, the world, and people's day-to-day existence."

Does John Paul II overrate the difficulties of transitional crises? Even he cannot and will not offer specific solutions for them. His deepest cause for worry are not political and social systems themselves, but the fact that they all have more or less drawn away from the moral message of Christianity. For the pope, the true measure of their value is the degree to which they are secularized. His hopes and fears cannot be reduced to a common denominator, and that is both his weakness and his strength. This pope, who always closes his eyes when he prays, is neither yogi nor commissar. He steps back behind his office even as it drives him further out into the world. When he assumed his pontificate in 1978, he had the traditional epithet following his name, *felicemente regnante*—happily reigning—struck from the papal chronicle.

Thrust onto the vast stage of world history, Pope John Paul II took up his pontificate without theatrics but also with no sign of stage fright, in the firm conviction that he had been chosen by Providence. His pontificate would become one of the longest in history. Many chose not to follow his call, and his sharpest critics would come from the Catholic camp. But millions around the world were fascinated by the new Polish pope, and to every corner of the world he would carry the message he proclaimed shortly after his election: "Have no fear! Open your gates, yes, tear them open wide for Christ! Open your national borders, your economic and political systems, your broad areas of culture and of progress to his saving power!"

Preservation and Forgiveness—The Attempted Assassination in Rome

May 13, 1981. Before the eyes of the world the unthinkable happened. An attempt on the life of John Paul II. In the middle of St. Peter's Square, Mehmet Ali Agca aimed his pistol at the pope, riding past in an open car, and fired three shots. Badly wounded, the pope collapsed and was rushed to Rome's Gemelli Clinic. He survived, but his health would never be the same. Repeated operations were required. Ali Agca was captured, arrested, and sentenced to a long prison term. But to this day the attack has never been fully explained. Was it part of some secret-service plot? The act of a deluded loner? The pope later visited Ali Agca in prison and forgave him. To John Paul II, his preservation is part of a larger context. On May 13, 1917, three shepherd children in Fatima, Portugal, had a vision of the Virgin and were given coded apocalyptic messages. Veneration of the Virgin experienced a dramatic upsurge as a result, and soon there was talk of the "three secrets of Fatima." The first is supposed to have predicted the outbreak of World War I, the second that of World War II. The third secret remained unknown for decades. John Paul II interpreted his rescue on May 13, 1981, as the result of Mary's intervention—"one hand shot, and another guided the bullet"—thereby establishing a connection to Fatima. The attempt on his life is said to have been foretold in the third prophecy. The bullet that was removed from the pope's body is now in Fatima, incorporated into a radiant crown atop the statue of the Virgin.

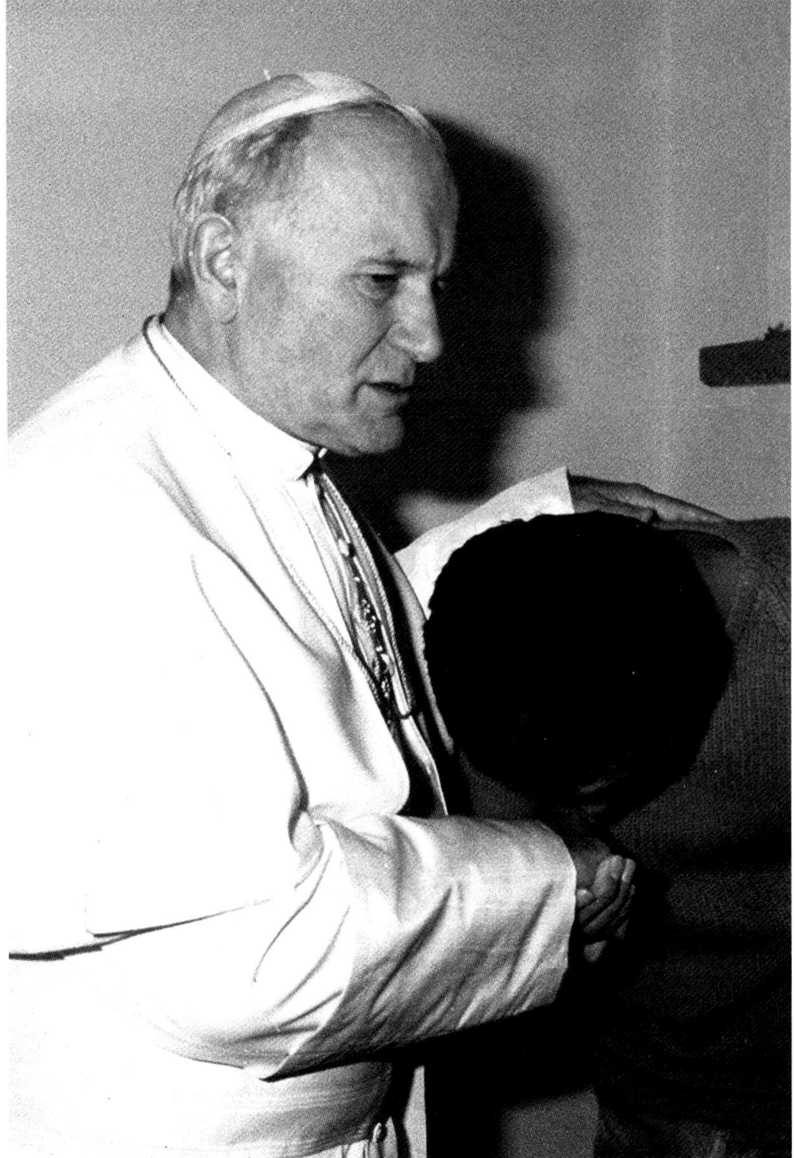

Arthur Hertzberg

THE POPE AND THE JEWS

Throughout his papacy, John Paul II has returned again and again to several central issues. He has fought, and won, a relentless battle against the power of Communism in Central and Eastern Europe. He has fought, and lost, the battle to keep the whole Catholic Church within the bounds of its orthodox doctrines. A majority of his flock of perhaps a billion people is far more liberal in its sexual practices than the pope insists that they must be. This massive disregard of his teachings calls into question the central affirmation of his theology: the *magisterium*—the supreme authority—of the Church, and of popes, past and present. One other issue has clearly consumed John Paul II: the connection between Catholics and Jews, and here his labors have made enormous changes for the good, though they have also left questions and irritations in their wake.

How can the Jews of the world, and the overwhelming majority of the decent people within the Catholic community, not admire a pope who was the first to pay a formal visit to the synagogue in Rome in 1986; who led the Church to establish formal relations with the state of Israel in 1994; and who condemns and has repeatedly expressed remorse for anti-Semitism, past and present? And yet, how can the Jews be completely comfortable with a pope who was the only head of state to receive a political and moral pariah, President Kurt Waldheim of Austria, at the Vatican in 1987 with full honors, even though Waldheim was being boycotted by other world leaders? In the 1980s Yasir Arafat, the leader of the Palestine Liberation Organization, had not uttered the slightest denunciation of Palestinian terrorist assaults on Israeli civilians, but this pope received him at the Vatican as a statesman of consequence.

John Paul II has created more saints than any pope in history, and this enthusiasm has led him to at least two controversial canonizations. The most famous is his canonization of a convert from Judaism, the Carmelite nun Santa Theresa (Edith Stein). The pope insisted that she was, indeed, a martyr to her Jewishness and, above all, to her Christian faith. Jews have countered that the Nazis did not send her and her sister to Auschwitz, where they were killed on the day of their arrival, because they were Christians, but because they were Jews. An equally pointed and by now somewhat forgotten battle was waged with the Church, and with this pope, over the beatification of the Polish priest Father Maximilian Kolbe. The priest had sacrificed his life in Auschwitz to save a Polish layman who had been sentenced to die of starvation as a deterrent for others after the successful escape of a fellow prisoner. This man cried that he was the head of a family and the father of a number of children. Kolbe, hearing the outcry, volunteered to replace him. Paradoxically, however, in the 1930s Kolbe had been editor of one of the most anti-Semitic publications in Poland. Based on this past, he seemed to be the very incarnation of the bitter anti-Semitism that marked the Polish Church in the 1930s, of which an overt

"Christ cannot be shut out of human history. At no latitude or longitude." It is this conviction that has caused Pope John Paul II to restlessly roam the world—in terms of miles traveled, he has circled the globe roughly twenty-nine times. He has visited 129 of the world's 194 countries, and not a few heads of government have hoped that a papal visit might help to shore up their authority. By others, even the Vatican's request for an official invitation has been perceived as an open threat. To millions of the faithful—like this nun—his visits have simply been gripping celebrations of faith, highly emotional encounters that no one would want to miss.

P. 64

John Paul II's installation on October 22, 1978.

anti-Semite, Cardinal August Hlond, was then the primate. Nonetheless the attack on the beatification of Kolbe was ill-informed and unfair. He had been deported to Auschwitz in 1941 because the Gestapo discovered that he had hidden people, including Polish army officers and many Jews. Surely, his courage and charity at the end counted toward his canonization by John Paul II.

These irritations between John Paul II and the Jewish community are not the only ones. Indeed, they indicate that this pope is not, in the mind of many Jews, of one piece, and they do not understand what seemed to them to be his ambivalences. The issue came to a head in 1987 when John Paul II was on a visit to a number of cities in Latin America and the southeastern United States. His first stop in the United States was Miami. He was eager to follow his usual custom of receiving, among the many delegations that normally crowded his antechamber, representatives of the major Jewish organizations in the United States. That was not to be, however, because the organized Jewish community was furious with the pope for having received Austria's Waldheim. The leaders of American Jewry had no intention of appearing to legitimize this action by meekly meeting with the pope. The Vatican, clearly upset by the turn of events, even sent the cardinal secretary of state, Agostino Casaroli, to New York to see what he could do to end the boycott. This effort met with some success. A few rabbis and laymen were found who would meet the pope. The Vatican was so grateful for this meeting that a few years later it honored the most prominent of these rabbis with a knighthood of the Order of St. Gregory. Nonetheless, this meeting could not truly be described as a success for the Church. On the contrary, it made quite clear that John Paul II would have to take account of the issues important to the international Jewish community.

What are the deepest issues in the heart and mind of this pope who grew up among Jews in a small town in Poland? All of his biographers emphasize that Karol Wojtyla, as a young schoolboy in Wadowice, was not an anti-Semite. His father, too, was very pronouncedly on the other side of politics of the day. Karol had Jewish friends, including one very close friend, Juri Kluger, among his schoolmates. Kluger and Wojtyla spent much time in each other's homes, doing schoolwork together, and Karol Wojtyla often volunteered to play on the "Jewish team" in its encounters with the "Catholic team" at school. Both Wojtyla and Kluger graduated high school in 1938. Wojtyla went off to Kraków to enter the university there; Kluger's future was more uncertain because university admission was in those days extremely difficult for a Jew to attain. On September 1, 1939, the Germans invaded Poland and the destiny of each young man was radically affected. Kluger and his father fled eastward to try to find a Polish army unit to which they could attach themselves. Wojtyla left the university because he had no money and found a job working in a quarry.

He became very involved in underground Polish nationalist theatrical endeavors as a form of resistance to the Nazis, who wanted to stamp out all expressions of Polish nationalism; what the young Karol Wojtyla—who turned twenty in May of 1940—did not do was join any of the efforts to save Jews from being murdered in the streets of Kraków or being deported by the Nazis to concentration camps such as Belzec, in eastern Poland, not far from Lvov, or to Auschwitz, some forty miles away from Kraków.

There can be no doubt about this because if he had been involved in any of the efforts to save Jews, his biographers would have lauded such endeavors. George Weigel and Tad Szulc, his two friendliest biographers, have simply avoided the subject. More revealing, the pope was once asked, on camera by an interviewer, a point-blank question: What did you do to help Jews during the Nazi era? With pain in his face, he answered with one word: nothing. It is more than surprising that Karol Wojtyla, as he began rising in the church to become bishop of Kraków and then archbishop and cardinal, did not search for any of his old Jewish friends from his school days. In fact, one of them, who reestablished relations with Wojtyla, saw a newspaper interview with me some years ago in which I discussed this puzzle, that a man who had warm relations with Jews from the beginning of his life had been so inactive as the Holocaust was happening before his eyes. This survivor (I promised that I would never reveal his name) contacted me to say that the pope's behavior in those early days continued to trouble him. I continue to ask myself, if he knew that the lives of women and children of some of the Jewish families in Wadowice were in danger during the most murderous of years, 1942 and 1943, could he think of no room in Kraków where he could hide at least a few of them?

Toward the end of the war Karol Wojtyla had to hide in the basement of the archiepiscopal palace in Kraków in fear that the Nazis would find and punish him, or even destroy him, for his Polish nationalist and Catholic religious activities. No doubt, this is what Pope John Paul II will offer as explanation when, speaking in Polish, he explains himself before the heavenly court, but I am certain that even on that very day his soul will continue to be troubled by the memory of what he might have done for Jews—for his friends among them—in their time of greatest need. He has done much to rid the Church of anti-Semitism and to build bridges to the Jewish people, but has he yet forgiven himself for those years in which he could have done more?

When Karol Wojtyla became Pope John Paul II in 1978 there were some vehement right-wing cranks who chose to imagine that this new pope was arriving from Poland laden with Communist teachings. He was, some said, a plant from the enemies of Western society. These ideologues persisted in

Beneath the gaze of the Black Madonna of Częstochowa, Poland, in June 1979.

believing this for some years, even as the pope's policies and demeanor proved otherwise. He began his papacy by working tirelessly to undermine the Communist regime in his native Poland and to support the revolt that had begun with the strike of the shipbuilders in Gdańsk, the Solidarity movement led by Lech Walesa. This was hardly the activity of a Communist agent disguised in the vestments of a pope. This pope was totally free from and opposed to the anti-Semitic traditions of the Polish church, but, in all other respects, he was the heir of its most orthodox version of the Catholic faith. His definition of being a Catholic constrained him to look at all of the problems of the world within the limits of Catholic theology.

Even on the Jewish question he could not allow himself to go beyond these limits. In human terms it would have been much easier for him to believe, and to say, that Pope Pius XII had not behaved as well as he should have during the Nazi years. He could even have added that he, too, had much to regret, but never in his many statements on Jews and Judaism, on the Holocaust and anti-Semitism, has John Paul II ever gone this far. To do so would mean an admission that the Church is not perfect. The Orthodox Catholic who is now the inhabitant of the chair of St. Peter, the Bishop of Rome, and the "universal bishop" of the Catholic Church simply could not apologize for the Church. On the contrary, he constructed and often restated a position that is diametrically opposed to the view of many Jews. The pope maintains that individual Christians who had been baptized as Catholics might have contravened the will of God and behaved badly, but Pope Pius XII, and especially the Church, are pure and unsullied. The dominant Jewish view is precisely the reverse: the Church as a whole—the Church that excommunicated the Communists but never the Nazis—was sinful; some of its adherents, among both the clergy and the laity, behaved with heroic and self-sacrificing virtue. For them the Jews are eternally grateful, but these individuals did not save the honor of the Church as an institution.

On the innumerable occasions when John Paul II has spoken of the Holocaust—the murder of the Jews by the Nazis and their helpers—he has been especially moved, and both angry and contrite. He has even added to the Catholic liturgy and prayer begging Divine forgiveness for the inhumanity that was shown to the Jews. Nonetheless, every one of his declarations described the assault on the Jews as the action of individuals who had abandoned their faith in God. He is even willing to concede that some of these individuals were encouraged by their false understanding of Christian teaching, but the Church and its dogma were not in any way guilty of this sin.

This Catholic orthodoxy has deeply affected the ongoing battle over access to the diplomatic record of Pius XII's papacy. Let us lay aside the Vatican's oft-repeated excuses that the documents that stem from the activities of Pius XII are not yet adequately catalogued, or that it must wait fifty years after the death of the pope in question to release the papers. The Vatican has already broken this rule by publishing eleven volumes describing its diplomatic activities during the Nazi years, and these volumes are almost completely silent on the information that is known to have poured in, most certainly after the middle of 1942, about the scale of the Nazi murders of Jews. The documents in these eleven volumes have clearly been edited to obscure what the Vatican surely knew, that the Jews were being murdered en masse. Even if the archives were made available, does anyone really think that they have not been cleansed of anything that might prove damaging or embarrassing? Therefore, what difference does it make whether full access, whatever that may mean, is granted? The question of Pius XII and the Holocaust has essentially ceased being a focus for scholars. For Catholics, it has entered the realm of theology: no pope can be made to sit on the bench of the morally accused. For Jews, it is firmly embedded in their remonstration: the Church was the one moral force in Europe that might have saved many of their brothers and sisters; how can it continue to speak of love when it chose instead to protect itself? This argument will not end anytime soon.

In recent years some Jews and Catholics have suggested it would be better to move beyond the debate about Pius XII and assessing blame for the horrible events of sixty years ago, and instead move toward the good that we can do for the future. There are now even some leaders in the Jewish community who are willing to accept the good that John Paul II has done and give him the right to insist, despite repeated objections from some Jews, that Pius XII be canonized, especially if such action is linked with the canonization of the most beloved of all papal figures of recent history, John XXIII. While not yet a majority opinion, one suspects that ultimately it will prevail. The Jewish community knows that, despite his ambivalences, this pope has been, and remains, a friend—one of the greatest friends that Jews have ever had among the occupants of the papacy.

The most difficult part of John Paul II's life to assess fairly and convincingly is the account of his early adult years. It is beyond doubt that he had close friends among his Jewish classmates in the public high school that he attended in his native village of Wadowice and that he is indeed, as he himself has told with some pride, the first modern

"Can man expect after the experiences of the concentration camps, gulags, bomb attacks... something even worse—still more humiliation, contempt, despair? In a word: a hell?" John Paul II's meetings with concentration camp survivors (as here during his first trip to Poland) have proved shattering to him. The "absence of God" would be the obverse of a universal faith in Christ. How can a good and all-powerful god permit so much suffering, a hell on earth? The pope chooses to see God's involvement in even the most abysmal suffering, and has referred to the agony and death of Christ over and over again. To many Jews, such analogies are an inadmissible "appropriation" of their pain.

pope to have a personal connection to the Jewish community and to have acquired substantial awareness of Jewish practices and beliefs. The building in which he lived with his widowed father was close to the local synagogue, and John Paul II still remembers images of Jews coming in and out of the synagogue on the Sabbath and Jewish holidays, dressed in their best. After high school, the young Karol Wojtyla moved to Kraków where he supported himself by working in a stone quarry. In his free time, he was a leading member of an amateur group of actors who performed Polish nationalist plays. This endeavor had been forbidden by the Nazis, who were repressing expressions of nationalism, but Karol and his friends persisted. He was also involved, ever more deeply, in his religious faith. He continued with his studies in philosophy at Kraków University, but entered a secret seminary in Kraków when he decided to become a priest. Some have suggested that during the war years he belonged to a group that had put the helping of Jews in its charter but no specifics of personal action by the young Wojtyla have ever been offered in the copious biographical literature. Wojtyla certainly knew of active resistance to the Nazis, including taking the risk of hiding Jews, because a fellow seminarian who was caught doing exactly that was shot by the Nazis.

It seems evident that the memory of his silence during the Holocaust did make Wojtyla uncomfortable. As a young prelate, he began to intervene for Jews. Early in his career a woman came to him with a small child, a girl. The woman wanted to baptize the child. It only took a few moments for Father Wojtyla to determine that the child had been left with the woman by the girl's mother, a Jew who was about to be transported to Auschwitz by the Nazis. Father Wojtyla insisted that the woman who had saved the baby's life was not free to make the choice that she be baptized as a Christian. This baby needed to be returned to what remained of her family. This story has been confirmed by a Jewish woman who now lives in California; she has said that she was that baby girl.

"I come here today as a pilgrim. As you know, I have often been here before—and how often! And many times I have descended into the death cell of Maximilian Kolbe, have stood before the wall of death, and have clambered about the ruins of the crematoriums at Birkenau. I could not omit a visit here as pope... so I have come, and I kneel at this Golgotha for our time, before these graves, most of which bear no name, just like the grave of the unknown soldier. I kneel before all the plaques that form such a long row, and on which the memory of the victims of Auschwitz is recorded in the following languages: Polish, English, Bulgarian, Romany, Czech, Danish, French, Greek, Hebrew, Yiddish, Spanish, Flemish, Serbo-Croatian, German, Norwegian, Russian, Romanian, Hungarian, and Italian. Finally, I pause with you before the plaque inscribed in Hebrew. It brings to mind that people whose sons and daughters were destined for complete extermination. This people traces its faith back to Abraham, the 'father of our faith,' as Paul of Tarsus put it. Of all people, this one that received from God the commandment "Thou shalt not kill!" was forced to experience firsthand to an extraordinary degree what killing means. No one can pass this memorial unmoved."

JOHN PAUL II IN AUSCHWITZ IN 1979

Very little about Wojtyla's connection to the Jews of Kraków is known for certain. Immediately after he was elected pope in 1978, the Jewish Telegraphic Agency, the semiofficial news source for the worldwide Jewish community, published a report in its October 26 issue that Wojtyla had kept the Jews of Kraków at a distance. His former aides told the interviewers that "the Cardinal also never met...with surviving Polish Jews or visiting Jewish delegations." His former secretary added that "the Cardinal never had the opportunity to meet Jews." The conclusion of the JTA account was "that the new pope has up till now refrained, voluntarily or for lack of interest, from contact with Jews in Poland or abroad.... He has also never shown any apparent interest in the Holocaust and the martyrdom of Poland's Jews except within the wider concept of 'human persecutions.'"

Two of the Jewish organizations that had a major and continuing interest in good relations with the Vatican could not let this assessment go unanswered. On November 2, the Anti-Defamation League released a report from its representative in Rome, Dr. Joseph L. Lichten. He asserted that during the Nazi occupation Karol Wojtyla had assisted Jews in finding shelter and acquiring false papers identifying them as "Aryan." After the war, according to Lichten, the young Father Wojtyla helped to arrange for the permanent care of the Jewish cemetery in Kraków. When he became bishop, the diocesan weekly in Kraków devoted more space to Jews than any other in Poland. This friendly account of John Paul II's earlier years was, in fact, preceded by a week or two by a press release issued by Rabbi Marc H. Tanenbaum, who was then the national director of interreligious affairs of the American Jewish Committee. Tanenbaum praised the future pope for having denounced the vandalism in Jewish cemeteries in Kraków in 1964. These desecrations were attributed to the agents of the Polish Communist Party and the secret police (and not to a more likely source, the Polish nationalist anti-Semites). The then-Archbishop Wojtyla's public persona was consonant with his attributing this outrage to the Communists. Rabbi Tanenbaum also told that in 1971, four years after becoming a cardinal, Wojtyla came to the synagogue in Kraków for a Friday night Sabbath service and was sympathetic to the problems of the small community. These statements from Jewish sources were not entirely divorced from Jewish needs. It was regarded as prudent to suggest that the new pope who was coming on the international scene in 1978 was not indifferent to Jews, but was someone who had a record of friendship with them. They had

Larger than life-size. For Pope John Paul II the cross stands at the center of his theological reflections. The cross, a truly Christian symbol that is interpreted comprehensively and in cosmic terms: the cross symbolizes salvation, life, and hope. Here it looms above an altar constructed at Le Bourget, France, in June 1980.

probably colored the facts about Wojtyla's past, but in the big picture they were right. John Paul II was never an enemy. Now that he was pope, he would work hard at being a friend.

Within a year of his ascension to the pontificate, John Paul II visited Auschwitz, in 1979, where he called the Holocaust "this Golgotha for our time." The single most important turning point in his relationship to Jews and to Judaism came in 1986 when he visited the synagogue in Rome, thus becoming the first pope to enter a Jewish religious building and take part in what amounted to a joint religious service, led alternately by him and the chief rabbi of Rome. Three years later, in 1989, the Pontifical Commission for Peace and Justice denounced anti-Semitism "as the most tragic form that racist ideology has assumed in our century." John Paul II has been so concerned about anti-Semitism that he has even been willing to admit that some Christian teachings, based on "erroneous and unjust" interpretations of the New Testament, were part of the foundation of the anti-Semitism that led to the Holocaust. In January 1995, on the fiftieth anniversary of the liberation of Auschwitz, he described the Holocaust "as a darkening of reason and of the heart." The year before, John Paul II did what he had been hinting for a number of years that he would do: he established formal diplomatic relations between the Vatican and the state of Israel.

Thus sixteen years after this Polish churchman had become pope, the Jews of the world could feel that their major objectives in dialogue with the Roman Catholic Church had been achieved: the Church had abandoned and denounced anti-Semitism, forbidding the various versions of the catechisms from repeating attacks on Jews, and the Church had found a way to recognize the state of Israel, not as an answer to messianic hopes, but as an acceptable secular state that has as much right to exist as any other. Yet it remained clear that the Jews of the world were not unanimous, or even nearly so, in hailing John Paul II as the successor of John XXIII. There was even the feeling in certain circles that John Paul II reminded some Catholics, and some Jews, of Pius XII. The interpretation was offered in both communities that this is a man divided within himself: he was reaching out to all of humanity, and especially to the Jews who had so long been persecuted, but he still carried the responsibility for the future of the Church as an institution.

I do not believe that this interpretation is correct or that it does justice to John Paul II. He is one man, not two. Everything that he has said and done fits into his conception of what the teachings and the interest of the Catholic Church permit. Thinking about the Jews, he has gone to the very end of Catholic orthodoxy as he perceives it, but never beyond. Even on the most painful of subjects, anti-Semitism and its ultimate expression in his own lifetime, the Holocaust, nothing that he has ever said or done has broken beyond the limits of his orthodoxy.

In this connection, one needs to understand correctly an issue that troubled the Jewish-Catholic relationship in the 1980s and into the early 1990s: the existence of a Carmelite nunnery on the grounds of Auschwitz. Jews saw this as a desecration. They were resolute in their belief that the Auschwitz complex, in which the majority of those murdered were Jews, should best be left without any religious symbolism; it should remain a place of desolation. The many hundreds of thousands of Jews who were murdered there certainly did not need Christian prayers by pious nuns to improve their status in heaven. Because the Polish Church supported the nuns, the existence of this nunnery became an international issue. The Vatican made the decision in 1989 that the nunnery must be moved to a place outside of Auschwitz, and that a field of crosses that had been erected near their building should be taken down. This did not happen. The pope himself finally had to intervene in 1993, decreeing that the removal must be carried out. He appeared to be taking the side of those who were protesting the preemption by a nunnery of the religious presence at this horrible place—but it was not quite the whole story. A large cross, which the pope himself had blessed on one of his visits to Auschwitz, was left as the sole religious symbol standing there. John Paul II did not go the whole journey; he left in place the cross, explaining to his flock that all that had happened in Auschwitz was a reenactment of the suffering of Jesus on the cross of Golgotha. He could no more let go of this notion than he could admit that the convert from Judaism, Edith Stein, had been sent to Auschwitz because she was a Jew; John Paul II insisted that this Jewish woman died as a martyr to the Catholic faith. But what had Edith Stein ever done, except for having been born a Jew, that had made her more of a candidate for being gassed in Auschwitz than thousands of other nuns in Nazi-occupied Europe?

The same fundamental theme, great human sympathy for the suffering of the Jews but unrelenting defense of the record of the Church, has marked John Paul II's treatment of anti-Semitism. He has consistently attributed the presence of Jew-hatred in Christian teaching and among so many Christians through the ages to the misinterpretations of the New Testament by individual Catholics and the unforgivable errors of some laymen, and many millions of others, past and present. The Church itself has been repeatedly held up by John Paul II as the pure and immaculate bride of Christ. In recent history, John Paul II has maintained, the Church was the major force for saving hundreds of thousands of Jews. No one has yet produced a justification for this claim. It is true that there were churchmen and churchwomen and Catholic believers of all kinds who risked their lives to protect Jews from death at the hands of the Nazis. In fact, more than five thousand such people are commemorated in a grove of trees on the grounds of Yad Vashem, the main Holocaust memorial in

Jerusalem. But higher up in the Catholic hierarchies, both in the Vatican and in most of the countries in Europe, the numbers of the defenders of the Jews were few. John Paul II cannot attribute theological anti-Semitism to the teaching of the Church but only to some who were in error. He cannot accept the assertion that the honor of the Catholic faith was saved during the Holocaust not by the Vatican and most of the hierarchies in Europe but by heroic individual Catholics.

The most pointed confrontation between John Paul II and dominant Jewish opinion is in the continuing battle over the legacy of Pius XII. It is an open secret that the proceedings for the canonization of John XXIII are stalled in the Vatican by the difficulties over canonizing Pius XII. John Paul II insists that his predecessor did everything within his power to protect Jews during World War II. But this issue continues to burn within Jewish hearts. This conflict was made evident to John Paul II at the single most dramatic moment of his attempt to reconcile with the Jews, when he was the first pope in history to visit a synagogue, where his hosts were the chief rabbi in Rome, Elio Toass, and the lay head of the Jewish community, Professor Giacomo Saban. In his address of welcome, Professor Saban asserted that the central synagogue and St. Peter's Cathedral were on opposite sides of the famed historic river, the Tiber. Professor Saban then added:

> What was taking place on one of the banks of the Tiber could not have been unknown on the other side of the river, nor could what was happening elsewhere on the European continent.

The pope said some very moving things that day about the relationship between Jews and Christians—Jews are our older brothers, the first children of the patriarch Abraham—but he did not respond to the remark about the silence of Pius XII when the Jews of Rome were being rounded up and deported. John Paul II could not respond, and not simply because he was defending the reputation of Pius XII.

Among the many saints whom John Paul II has canonized is Pius IX. In the

A militant pope. Energetic and dynamic. Uncompromising. Aggressive. And not a few are offended by him. Even within the Church there are opposing camps—here the conservatives, there the progressives. Among the debated issues: his strict morality regarding sex and marriage, his exclusion of women from the priesthood and ministry, his controversial appointment of bishops, the behavior of the Congregation for the Doctrine of the Faith toward theology professors. In the liberal media it was soon the unanimous perception that John Paul II was guiding the Church in a conservative, doctrinaire fashion. Even so, he is by no means the fanatic holy warrior many make him out to be. He has been untiring in his struggle for human rights, uncompromising in his defense of peace and justice, forthright in his recognition that in the history of his Church there have been mistakes and injustices. After his first hundred days, under the headline "Progressivism of a Conservative," the Swiss newspaper *Neue Zürcher Zeitung* said of him: "For as long as anyone can remember, the first well-trained theologian in the Holy See." This picture was taken during a speech in Paris in 1980.

TOW AWAY ZONE
WALLACK
POLICE
POLICE

GREATER NEW YORK SAVINGS
ONE WAY

"For a week the Pope drowned out the din of America's consumer culture. More than ten million Americans of every race, every faith, and every age had a direct experience of the pilgrim from Rome at the six stops on his U.S. trip: Boston, New York, Philadelphia, Des Moines, Chicago, and Washington. And it is impossible to guess how many followed the almost continuous live coverage on television and radio. The newspapers devoted many pages to the visit day after day. *The New York Times*, owned by a Jewish family, printed on its front page the liturgical text of the celebration of the Eucharist with the Pope in Yankee Stadium, and also printed a photograph across the entire width of its front page for the first time ever. U.S. observers commented that no event, not even the first moon landing, had so captured and held the public's attention and caused the media to deploy such forces and such technology as the papal visit. Yet the Pope's message was a challenge to the American way of life, to the self-centeredness of this leading Western power caught up in purely materialistic pursuits...." Such was the report of the Vatican Information Service on October 11, 1979. After his statement of principles to the United Nations, the pope included the president and later Nobel Peace Prize–winner Jimmy Carter in his prayer: "The United States of America bears a heavy responsibility for the creation of a just and humane world, precisely because it has such a high standard of living and has achieved such a high degree of technological development."

THE PHOTOGRAPHS

Parade up Manhattan's Madison Avenue (pp. 80–81); joking with President Jimmy Carter outside the White House (p. 82); during a speech in a windy New York City (p. 83); triumphal entry into Washington, D.C. (p. 85).

history of the Church, Pius IX is significant because he was the pope during the last third of the nineteenth century who declared war on all aspects of modern culture. He commended authority and abhorred democracy; he vastly increased the Index, the list of books that were forbidden. The world he condemned is essentially the world in which most Westerners find themselves living. To canonize Pius IX was essentially a denunciation of all those who would challenge or question the authority of any pope. The message is that anyone who once denies what a pope decrees about the meaning of the faith is approaching heresy. One could, therefore, be sympathetic to the suffering of Jews only to the degree to which their claim to sympathy did not contradict this fundamental teaching.

Despite all of his sympathy for Jews, John Paul II was not deterred from canonizing Pius IX even after learning of the case of Edgardo Mortara. Mortara, whose family was Jewish, was taken from his parents at the age of six in June 1858 because the housekeeper had secretly baptized him five years before. Despite a large outcry against this act, Pius IX refused all the petitions to return the child to his parents. Later, in 1870, when the Church no longer controlled the papal states, the young Mortara was free to return to his family and to Judaism, but he refused to do so. By this time, he had become an ardent Catholic who spearheaded some of the efforts to convert Jews. Mortara died in 1940 in Belgium. Perhaps the difference between this instance and that of the children of Jewish origin who had been saved by Christian foster parents—whom the young Bishop Wojtyla had made give back to their families—was that no baptism had taken place; Mortara had been baptized, and therefore John Paul II could uphold the orthodox doctrine of Pius IX: the child had become a Catholic forever.

John Paul II has never, to my knowledge, used the contemporary technical term among theologians, "supercession," to define the role of the Church as the last step in the unfolding of God's revelation to mankind. In this version, Jews are indeed the ones who received the Old Testament, which the New Testament has "corrected," and yet, even in some of his statements to Jews, John Paul II has consistently asserted that the cross over Auschwitz is the symbol that includes all who suffered.

Even in the basic proclamation of 1964, *Nostra Aetate*, on the relationship of the Catholic Church to other faiths, the primacy of Christianity is asserted:

> The Catholic Church rejects nothing of what is true and holy in these religions. She has a high regard for the manner of life and conduct, the precepts and doctrines which, although differing in many ways from her own teaching, nevertheless often reflect a ray of that truth which enlightens all men. Yet she proclaims and is duty bound to proclaim without fail. Christ who is "the way, the truth and the life" (John 14:6).

John Paul II could not think of straying from this assertion. Indeed, he explains the Holocaust in Christological terms. Speaking to Jewish leaders in Warsaw in 1987, John Paul II said:

> It was you who suffered this terrible sacrifice of extermination. One might say that you suffered it also on behalf of those who were in the purifying power of suffering. The more atrocious the suffering, the greater the purification.

Believers in other faiths are not comforted by this Christian vision. John Paul II's Christian faith and his early experiences in Wadowice have moved him to contrition and to the desire to make a fresh start, but this will not happen so long as the best of non-Christians, the believers who share his passion for peace and justice, are being told by this pope that in some mysterious way they have already found their way to Jesus. In my most spiritual moments, I keep trying to find my way not to the cross that once stood on Golgotha but to my Jewish ancestors who have practiced their faith in often trying circumstances.

At the encounter in the synagogue in Rome, John Paul II and the president of the Jewish community were essentially talking past each other. Even as the pope made the most respectful gesture that he could to Jews and Judaism, he still had to emphasize that the correct culmination of the Jewish experience was in Jesus and that the greatest value that Christianity cherished was the redeeming power of suffering. The very crowd that had come to the synagogue for this great event, many of whom remembered the tragedies and horrors that took place on their bank of the Tiber, was asserting its fundamental Jewishness: we are still here, despite the innumerable attempts to destroy us; our faith teaches us the courage to rebuild. I suspect that not many in that congregation could have quoted the Book of Job to the pope, but its teaching was deeply embedded within them. In the last verses of the tale of the disasters that had been heaped on Job, we are told that finally he came back to himself and found the strength to rebuild his family and his life. Catholics and Jews will come to peace with each other when they finally hear the teachings and intentions of each other's traditions. Let Catholics understand Jews, and let Jews hear Catholics, not as described in their own theologies but as Jews and Catholics see themselves. Then—and only then—can there be true peace among our faiths.

John Paul II considers Judaism an older brother to Christianity, and for that reason deplores the estrangement between the two that, elevated to righteous hatred, has left a bloody stain on history. While contemporary Jewish theologians generally have little to say about Christianity, John Paul II exploits every opportunity to recall the common root of both religions, the faith of Abraham.

In 1986 John Paul II became the first pope to enter a Jewish house of worship, the synagogue in Rome. This photograph shows him with Rabbi Elio Toaff. In the center, Cardinal Ugo Poletti.

Luigi Accattoli

A POPE WHO BEGS FORGIVENESS

John Paul II and His "Mea Culpa" at the Turn of the New Millennium

A pope begging forgiveness is the decisive innovation of John Paul II's pontificate and what will be most remembered. With his program of "conscience-probing at the end of the millennium" he has not only isolated himself to a large extent from the episcopate of the Catholic Church but also placed himself in pointed opposition to his Curia. To appreciate the true essence of this pontificate and its historic legacy it is therefore necessary to review his policy of soul-searching in some detail. On March 12, 2000, the pope could be seen kneeling in St. Peter's, kissing and embracing the crucifix, and begging forgiveness "for the faults of the sons and daughters of the Church past and present"—an image of John Paul II that historians will perhaps remember more than any other. The legacy of this Polish pope, who knows Marxism-Leninism like no other, is likely to be not so much his nationality but this act unprecedented in the history of the papacy.

The liturgy for that Sunday in March 2000 was to be a "confession of sins and plea for forgiveness." Seven representatives of the Roman Curia presented seven "invitatories" (invitations to prayer), to which the pope responded with seven "orations" (brief liturgical prayers). After a "confession of sins in general" there followed a "confession of sins committed in the service of truth," a "confession of sins which have harmed the unity of the body of Christ," a "confession of sins against the people of Israel," a "confession of sins committed in actions, love, peace, the rights of peoples, and respect for cultures and religions," a "confession of sins against the dignity of women and the unity of the human race," and finally a "confession of sins in relation to the fundamental rights of the person." Also remembered from that day are the dour faces of the cardinals and archbishops invited to share with the pope in this act of repentance: Bernardin Gantin (Benin), Joseph Ratzinger (Germany), Roger Etchegaray (France), Edward Cassidy (Australia), Stephen Fumio Hamao (Japan), Francis Arinze (Nigeria), and François-Xavier Nguyen Van Thuan (Vietnam).

The fourth of the seven confessions included a plea for forgiveness for persecution of the Jews: "God our Father, You have chosen Abraham and his descendants to carry your name to the nations: we are deeply saddened by the behavior of all those who in the course of history have caused your sons and daughters to suffer. We beg forgiveness and wish to commit ourselves to the reign of true brotherhood with the people of the Covenant." Two weeks later, on March 26 of the Jubilee year 2000, the pope

John Paul II is well aware that even Christians, "sons and daughters of the Church," have burdened themselves with profound guilt in the past and continue to do so today. With an eye to the Holy Year 2000, he began an unprecedented process of soul-searching, with frequent prayers for forgiveness that have occasioned more than one frown in Rome's Curia. Again and again his travels have taken him to the sites of unspeakable horrors, as here to Mauthausen, Austria, in 1988.

Poland 1983. The helicopter bearing the pope lifts away, the icon of the Madonna radiates a gentle calm, but the country is in ferment. In January 1981 John Paul II had received a delegation from the union Solidarity, and in December 1981 General Jaruzelski had imposed martial law throughout the country. The pope prayed publicly for Poland again and again. No direct allusions, no open tests of strength. But everyone could sense his protest. In the summer of 1983 he took his second trip as pope to Poland, with stops in Warsaw, Posen, Breslau, Kraków, and side trips to the pilgrimage sites of Częstochowa, St. Annaberg, and Piekary, in Upper Silesia. The city of Gdańsk, which the pope had originally hoped to visit, was denied him. Yet it was constantly present (p. 92). There was something unreal, almost mythical, about the pope's trip. General Jaruzelski would later formulate it in his memoirs as follows: "I am not a believer, to be sure, but a person still has some of it in him from his youth.... At that first encounter I had the vague sense of experiencing something stupendous." The writer Andrzej Szczypiorski recalls, "I saw him from afar, as in a bird's-eye view. I was standing right next to the upper rim of the stadium as he rode past below, next to the grass. Suddenly my vision started playing tricks on me, I was as though paralyzed, but it did not astonish me. I could see the Pope's face up close, as though through a strong telescope, also the faces of the other people, thousands of faces, each different, distinct, unlike any other. And I saw a wealth of color in the stadium that I had never noticed before, new, familiar colors existing sometime and somewhere but never seen in everyday, somnolent life."

By the time of the pope's third trip to Poland in 1987, Mikhail Gorbachev was at the helm in Moscow. The wind of change could no longer be denied. In Maidanek (pp. 99, 101) the pope again spoke of the Holocaust, and warned of a kind of blind nationalism oblivious to history. Yet after the changes in Eastern Europe, nationalism would flare up again, and not only in Poland.

GDAŃSK

carried this plea for forgiveness to God and to the Jews, written on a scrap of paper, to Jerusalem, and placed it in a crevice of the Wailing Wall.

The fivefold "never again" at the close of the service of repentance in St. Peter's constituted one of the strongest commitments to the spirit of the gospel ever formulated in our disenchanted epoch: "Never again opposition to love in the service of the truth, never again acts against the community of the Church, never again transgressions against any people, never again resort to the logic of power, never again discrimination, exclusion, suppression, neglect of the poor and the least."

John Paul II had announced his decision to make this "mea culpa" during the Great Jubilee back in 1993, but in fact the theme of "memory cleansing" most movingly expressed on that day runs through Karol Wojtyla's entire pontificate. From the "Galileo case"—John Paul II rehabilitated the astronomer, who had been condemned by the Inquisition in 1632—to the enslavement of blacks, from discrimination against women to the slaughter of the Huguenots in the St. Bartholomew Massacre, from Inquisition tribunals and the burning of heretics to the plundering of Constantinople during the Fourth Crusade—for some thirty wrongs this pope has prayed for forgiveness over the years. More than a hundred times he has admitted error or corrected an opinion expressed by Christians in the past, even earlier popes.

With this program the pope has extended the work of the Council in one important respect—that of reevaluating Church history in the light of modern knowledge—and perhaps has brought the Catholic congregation a major step closer to complete integration into the ecumenical movement. But he has also established a new apologetics, modified the image of the papacy (formerly seen as incapable of self-criticism), and redefined the position of the Catholic Church in the modern world. He has challenged the controversial orientation of Catholic apologetics, even reversed it, and placed it on a new foundation he feels is more appropriate to a culture of freedom and tolerance. This apologetics relies directly on the gospel. It is fully aware of the unavoidable breach between its claims and any hope for historical continuity, and sees the work of the faithful and of spiritual authorities (they, too, "sons and daughters of the Church") in its historical context.

Historically, the papal "mea culpa" is novel in two respects. Before John Paul II, only two popes in the entire history of the Catholic Church had admitted any historical guilt on the part of the Catholic Church and accepted responsibility for it: Hadrian VI (1522–1523) and Paul VI (1963–1978). But for these two, none of Pope John Paul II's predecessors ever called upon the Catholic congregation to examine its conscience and atone for past mistakes.

Pope Hadrian VI, a Dutchman, was the last non-Italian on the throne of St. Peter until John Paul II; he was followed, up until the election of

John Paul II, by forty-five Italian popes. In his brief pontificate, which spanned a mere thirteen months, Hadrian worked, despite resistance from the Curia, toward reconciliation with the Protestants in Germany. He announced a moral reform of the Curia, and admitted that his predecessors were responsible for "much that was abominable." The German princes nevertheless kept to their bond with Luther, and the reform pope died a short time later. It wasn't until the mid-twentieth century that another pope again embarked upon the path of admitting the Catholic Church's mistakes.

On September 29, 1963, at the opening of the second session of the Second Vatican Council, Pope Paul VI uttered the first "mea culpa" of our time when he turned toward representatives of Christian congregations that had separated from the Catholic Church and who were present in the council hall as observers: "If we are in any way guilty of such a separation, we humbly beseech God for forgiveness, and we also beg forgiveness from the brothers who felt injured because of us."

In the nearly five hundred years separating the pontificates of Hadrian VI and Paul VI, popes not only failed to admit present and past mistakes, they also expressly forbade the faithful from making such admissions. Examples of this can be found in the encyclical *Mirari Vos* (1832) of Pope Gregory XVI or the instructions from the Holy Office regarding the ecumenical movement from December 20, 1949. The belief was that the Church is sacred and the pope who interprets it infallible. Therefore, it cannot be their place to admit their own error or misconduct. It was only the Second Vatican Council, with its constitution on the Church drawn from biblical sources that made possible Karol Wojtyla's program of forgiveness. In that document, perhaps the most important of the Second Vatican Council, we read: "The Church, embracing in its bosom sinners, at the same time holy and always in need of being purified, always follows the way of penance and renewal" (*Lumen Gentium*, I, 8; 1964).

John Paul II's isolation on his path of soul-searching is explained by the fact that, historically, popes have been resistant to any form of self-criticism. If one considers the structure of the Catholic Church, its lines of authority, it becomes clear why only the pope could break this taboo of infallibility in the broad sense. Calling Church history to account, as Pope Wojtyla very deliberately has, means opposing the popes of the past. Only another pope can do that.

Owing to their fundamentally different structure, Protestant churches were able to make far-reaching confessions of sin long before Pope Paul VI's confession to the Second Vatican Council and those of John Paul II. That the breach in Christianity was a sin of which all churches are guilty was first admitted by bishops of the Anglican Church at the Lambeth Conference in 1920—more than forty years before the Second Vatican Council expressed a similar sentiment. Pronouncements like those of the

Anglican bishops followed in 1927 at the assembly of the Faith and Order Commission, in which representatives from both Protestant and Orthodox churches participated, and at meetings of the ecumenical Council of Churches in 1948 and 1954.

Yet the pope's plea for forgiveness at the turn of the new millennium not only stands in an ecumenical tradition and that of the Council, it springs from a personal need and from John Paul II's direct experience of the divisions between Christians during his pontificate—divisions that he flatly calls "sin," as on the occasion of a penitential liturgy in St. Peter's at the conclusion of the first European Synod on December 7, 1991: "The gospel exposes our sin, which we humbly acknowledge as the root of the present-day crisis in the Church."

The papal program of soul-searching and begging forgiveness is of enormous consequence. John Paul II's Polish origin may have made it easier for him to embark so determinately on this path of penitence. An Italian pope would doubtless have felt more strictly obligated to Roman tradition. And it is a considerable boon that the notion of begging forgiveness in the spirit of the gospel, so strongly resisted within the Church, was advanced by a pope no one could dream of accusing of failure to defend his faith.

John Paul II first mentioned the basic idea of declaring a historic soul-searching on the occasion of the Jubilee on the threshold of the new millennium. During an interview on November 2, 1993, with the Polish-Italian journalist Jas Gawronski, of the Italian daily *La Stampa*, he said, "To be sure, at the end of this millennium we must probe our conscience: Where do we stand, where has Christ led us, where have we diverged from the gospel?" The seed of this idea had been planted much earlier. His first self-critical statement relates to the Galileo issue, and dates from November 1979, at which point Pope Wojtyla had been in office scarcely a year. His efforts toward a general soul-searching were thus revealed long before he proclaimed a "Day of Pardon" as part of the celebration of the Great Jubilee, and continue far beyond that occasion. In the following I provide a chronological overview of the pope's most important confessions of sin during his pontificate, then examine more closely his program of soul-searching at the close of the millennium.

The Pope's Pleas for Forgiveness—First, the Galileo Case

John Paul II announced a reevaluation of the Galileo issue during a memorial celebration for Albert Einstein, while giving an audience to the Papal Academy of Sciences on November 10, 1979. The Second Vatican Council had already concerned itself with the Galileo case, and had apologized in Section 36 of the pastoral constitution *Gaudium et Spes* (1965), but without mentioning the scientist by name. His decision to discuss the case of Galileo once again attests to the pope's dissatisfaction with that apology, but also to his conviction that cleansing is possible and that all misunderstandings can be overcome: "Galileo—there is no denying it—suffered much pain at the hands of members and organs of the Church. The Second Vatican Council has admitted and apologized for improper interventions.... I request that theologians, scholars, and historians, fired with a spirit of honest collaboration, delve into the review of the Galileo case and in candid recognition of the injustice, no matter who was responsible, dispel the distrust that this episode continues to provoke in many minds regarding the fruitful collaboration between faith and science, the Church and the world."

A commission directed by Cardinal Paul Poupard, president of the Pontifical Council for Culture, was requested to again review the entire Galileo issue. In its closing report, submitted to the pope on October 31, 1992, the commission states: "Having inherited the unitary view of the world that prevailed up to the beginning of the seventeenth century, certain theologians of Galileo's time were in no position to fathom the deeper, non-literal meaning of the scriptures where they described the physical structure of the created universe. This led them to improperly transfer a question of determining facts to the realm of faith. In that historical and cultural context, which is far removed from our own, Galileo's judges believed that the acceptance of the Copernican revolution, which had not been definitely proved, moreover, would necessarily have the effect of undermining Catholic tradition, and that it was their duty to forbid its dissemination. This subjective error in judgment, so obvious to us today, led them to a disciplinary procedure under which Galileo had 'much to suffer.' These mistakes must be openly admitted—as you, Holy Father, have requested."

The language may be all too cautious in its references to "certain theologians" and "Galileo's judges." But the closing report does fundamentally recognize that the verdict of the Holy Office demanding that Galileo recant (1633) was owing to "mistaken judgment" and was thereby unjust with regard to the scientist, and that the Catholic Church must now "openly acknowledge" that the suffering imposed on him as a result was an offense and injustice on the part of the ecclesiastical authorities.

By October 1992 John Paul II was fully convinced that it was necessary to shed light on the "dark pages" of Church history. When he first spoke of the Galileo case in 1979, the feeling in Curia circles was that over time the pope would forget his initial decision to "acknowledge injustice" in the case of Galileo, or at least pursue it in modified form. But just the opposite was true: during the eleven years in which the commission investigated the Galileo issue, the pope carried out his own comprehensive investigations into comparable cases, especially in the course of his numerous journeys, which brought him into contact with knowledgeable

The pope in Częstochowa, Poland, in June 1983.

interlocutors all over the world. Not a year went by in which the pope did not speak self-critically.

On November 17, 1980, for example, at his meeting in Mainz with representatives of the German Council of the Evangelical Church, John Paul II called for a mutual admission of sin: "Today we can be aware that we are all in need of a fresh start.... Let us not judge each other, let us however confess to each other our guilt." In 1991 and again in 1995 he spoke insistently of the "sin" of the "breach between the churches." We will return to these statements later.

In Vienna on September 10, 1983, the pope spoke of the many wars in European history, all of them declared and fought by baptized Christians and often in the interest of conquest: "We must confess and beg forgiveness that we Christians have burdened ourselves with sin—in thought, word, and deed, and through passive indifference to injustice." In his apostolic letter of August 26, 1989, on the fiftieth anniversary of the outbreak of World War II, we hear a plaintive note that reveals what a long way John Paul II had come in only six years with regard to this issue, as historically dramatic as it was delicate in terms of Church politics: "The monstrous atrocities of that war took place on a continent...that has stood under the influence of the gospel and the Church longer than any other. It is truly difficult to carry on, knowing this horrifying Calvary of people and nations to be behind us."

On August 13, 1985, the pope addressed a meeting of academics and students in Yaoundé, in Cameroon, where he spoke heatedly against discrimination against blacks: "Over the course of history, people from Christian nations have not always [honored freedom and human rights], and we beg our African friends, who for example suffered so grievously under the slave trade, for forgiveness." On his trips to Africa Pope John Paul II has come back to this subject again and again. His most moving statement was during a visit to the "slave house" on Gorée Island, in Senegal, on February 22, 1992: "From this African shrine to black sorrow we implore the forgiveness of Heaven."

On April 13, 1986, on his visit to the synagogue in Rome, he deplored "all outbreaks of hatred, persecution, and manifestations of anti-Semitism directed against the Jews at any time by anyone, I repeat, by anyone." The pope was clearly referring here to his predecessors. Of his many other self-critical statements on the persecution of Jews in subsequent years let me mention only two: on June 23, 1996, he declared in Berlin that Catholics had done "too little" in defense of the Jews during the Shoah, and on October 31, 1997, speaking to participants in a colloquium on anti-Judaism, he stated that among many Catholics "their spiritual

General Jaruzelski and John Paul II in Warsaw in June 1987.

OPPOSITE AND PAGE 101
Maidanek, Poland, 1987.

opposition did not conform to what mankind might have rightly expected from the apostles of Christ."

In the United States in 1987 John Paul II once again spoke of the injustice done to Native Americans at the hands of colonists: "We must confess cultural suppression, iniquity, the destruction of your lives and your traditional societies. Sadly, not all members of the Church have done justice to their responsibility as Christians" (Phoenix, Arizona, meeting with North American Indians, September 14, 1987). The pope had already said much the same thing in 1984 in Canada, and in 1986 in Australia, in an attempt to clear away obstacles based on past injustices before speaking to these long-suffering peoples.

Rejection of Integralism

Since 1987 the pope has uttered numerous avowals of sin. On October 11, 1988, he gave an important speech to the European Parliament in Strasbourg in which he completely broke away from medieval integralism, the habit of popes in previous centuries to force Christian faith by state decree: "Medieval Latin Christianity never escaped the temptation to shut out from secular society those people who did not profess the true faith."

But even after this ceremonial declaration in Strasbourg, the pope himself was accused of integralism in his homeland of Poland, which had just escaped from Communist rule. On a trip to Poland in 1991, during which he called for the protection of life, he was subjected to highly direct and piercing attack. In a new declaration, he defended himself by saying, "The Church wishes to participate in the life of today's society solely as witness to the gospel, and all attempts to usurp any area of public life are foreign to it. A fanatical or fundamentalist posture is irreconcilable with Christian truth" (Olsztyn, June 6, 1991).

On June 5, 1991, the pope made an "admission of sin" for the split between the Eastern and Western churches during an ecumenical meeting in the Orthodox cathedral of Bialystok, in Poland: "We must concede that in relationships between our churches in the past the spirit of brotherhood preached by the gospel did not always prevail.... Wherever there was injustice, regardless on which side, it must be overcome by acknowledging one's own sins before God and through forgiveness."

In 1992, on the five hundredth anniversary of the evangelization of the New World, the pope journeyed a second time to Santo Domingo—a pilgrimage he called an "act of atonement" for the misdeeds of the colonists: "With this pilgrimage, a pilgrimage of thanks to the place where evangelization began, we also wished to perform an act of atonement before the infinite holiness of God for everything characterized by sin, injustice, and violence in this departure for the American continent.... We will not cease to beg these people for forgiveness. This plea for forgiveness is directed above all to the original inhabitants of the New World, to the Indians—and also to all those dragged here from Africa for forced labor as slaves" (general audience, October 21, 1992).

In 1994 the pope addressed a present-day injustice rather than an event from the past. On May 15 he spoke of the ethnic massacre raging in Rwanda at the time: "This is a true genocide, for which sadly even Catholics are responsible." With this it seems clear that John Paul II wished to counter any accusations that he only acknowledged past misconduct on the part of the Church.

On May 21, 1995, John Paul II visited Olomouc, in the Czech Republic, where he said: "Today I plead, the pope of the Church of Rome, in the name of all Catholics, for forgiveness for the wrong done to non-Catholics over the course of the sorrowful history of these peoples. At the same time, the Catholic Church forgives the evil that its children were forced to suffer." His choice of words attests to his intention to formulate a model declaration. On that day the Bohemian priest Jan Sarkander was canonized as a martyr. Sarkander had been condemned to death by Protestant authorities during the wars of religion that raged with particular devastation in Bohemia for 150 years. The Evangelical Church saw the canonization as a provocation, and some of its representatives stayed away from a meeting with the pope. Instead, they organized events commemorating Protestant "martyrs" condemned to death by Catholics. The pope's words must be read in this context. The world press called them brilliant, and Bohemian Protestants were abashed. With this symbolic gesture alone, the pope managed to defuse the situation. On his third visit to Prague, from April 25 to 27, 1997, John Paul II no longer met with such embittered resistance, and the Protestants no longer declined invitations to ecumenical gatherings.

Just over a month after he had "begged for forgiveness and granted forgiveness" in Olomouc, the pope brought about a similar turnaround in Slovakia. In Košice on July 2, 1995, he canonized as martyrs three priests who had been condemned to death by Protestant authorities in 1619. His proclamation offended local Protestants, who on the eve of the canonization gathered at a monument commemorating twenty-four Evangelical "martyrs" executed by Catholic authorities in Přerov in 1687. In his sermon in Košice the following morning, the pope recognized the "spiritual greatness" of the Protestant martyrs, and that afternoon he performed an astonishing gesture: he betook himself, in silence, on foot, and in the rain, to the monument to the Calvinist martyrs at the edge of the market square in Přerov's Old Town. There he was met by the Lutheran bishop of Přerov, Jan Midriak, who greeted him after a silent prayer and thanked him

for coming. Together they recited the Lord's Prayer. "We greatly appreciate this gesture," Midriak told journalists afterward. "We would never have dreamed that something like this could happen."

In that same year, 1995, John Paul II turned to Christians of the Eastern Church: "The sin of our separation weighs very heavily," he lamented. "We must apologize and entreat Christ for forgiveness.... We have deprived the world of a joint witness that could, perhaps, have avoided so many tragedies and even changed the course of history" (apostolic letter *Orientale Lumen*, May 2, 1995).

The mutual confession of sin by the pope and the Patriarch of Constantinople adopted this same tone. It attested to the fact that the pope was not alone on his path of repentance. "In the course of history and the most recent past there have been slights and acts of violence on both sides. While we beg the Lord for His abundant mercy, we invite all to forgive each other and manifest a new relationship of brotherhood and active collaboration" (Rome, joint declaration by John Paul II and Patriarch Bartolomeo I, June 29, 1995).

On the occasion of the Fourth International Women's Conference in 1995, John Paul II repeatedly referred to the situation of women and expressed his "regret" over the Church's behavior toward them: "I appeal to all men of the Church to undergo a change of heart if necessary and adopt a positive view of women as their faith commands" (message to the Vatican delegation to the International Women's Conference in Beijing on August 29, 1995).

In Paris on August 23, 1997, the pope recalled the St. Bartholomew's Massacre of 1572, which saw the slaughter of French Huguenots: "On the eve of the 24th of August one cannot forget the painful bloodbath of St. Bartholomew's night, occasioned by highly murky forces in the political and religious history of France. Christians committed acts condemned by the gospel." John Paul II thereby extended his hand to French Protestants, who had felt it a "provocation" on the part of the organizers of World Youth Day that the feast of St. Bartholomew was selected for the pope's meeting with young people. Protestants expressed their appreciation, and declared that it was now up to them to reflect on an episode in which mistakes were made on both sides.

On May 4, 2001, in Athens, the pope begged forgiveness for the plundering of Constantinople during the Fourth Crusade in 1204, when the Orthodox patriarch was forced into exile and replaced by a "Latin" one. Before his visit, the Orthodox community had stipulated that John Paul II needed to atone for this historic injustice. With his gesture of humility, at the end of the day Pope John Paul II managed to get members of the synod of Greek Orthodox churches to recite the Lord's Prayer with him, even though the protocol, at the request of the Orthodox, did not call for any joint liturgical acts. The objection had been that the two churches had not yet achieved "complete unity."

"Mea Culpa" at the Turn of the New Millennium

In the twenty-five years of his pontificate, John Paul II has issued more than a hundred self-critical statements, yet they by no means exhaust his pedagogy of forgiveness. His individual confessions of responsibility to history follow the path indicated by the Second Vatican Council and Pope Paul VI. John Paul II has made explicit what the Council implicitly admitted (Galileo); he has conveyed the messages the Council fathers included in their documents to their specific targets (Jews, Muslims, Orthodox and Protestant congregations); and he has applied what had already been stated in principle to new issues (the Inquisition, integralism, Indians, wars, discrimination against blacks and women). The pope has made nearly all his apologies while on his travels. In them one sees the missionary zeal of a man who, in getting his message to the people, senses the need to acknowledge the accountability of those who approached the people with the same message before him.

Wholly new, however, is the self-criticism in the spirit of the gospel that John Paul II has been practicing since 1993, which has no longer been primarily missionary in its motives but a kind of taking stock at the close of the millennium, culminating in his soul-searching and repentance in the Jubilee year 2000. In more recent addresses he has not been as concerned with clearing up misunderstandings and errors of the past as with preparing for the transition from the second to the third millennium in a spirit of "reconciliation and repentance." His conscience probing is wholly unprecedented in the Catholic tradition. For him, church history—a subject popes have always approached with the greatest of caution—has become a proving ground requiring extreme boldness.

His plan for such an examination of conscience is developed in the apostolic letter *Tertio Millennio Adveniente* (1994), one of the key texts of his pontificate and perhaps his most personal. The idea had already been formulated and discussed, however, in an extraordinary consistory, a full convocation of cardinals from around the world in the spring of 1994. That first proposal for an examination of conscience was a twenty-three-page *promemoria* that the pope presented to the consistory, titled *Reflections on the Great Jubilee of the Year 2000.* In Section 7 of that *promemoria*, under the heading "Reconciliatio et Paenitentia," the pope recommended taking "a searching look at the history of the second millennium" of the Church so as to "identify the errors…committed by its members." The title "Reconciliation and Repentance" recalls

FOLLOWING SPREAD

John Paul II has put some 720,000 miles behind him during his pontificate, on 102 separate trips abroad. In contrast to his predecessor Paul VI, who undertook only nine journeys to symbolically important places, John Paul II has visited a great majority of the countries in the world. This picture shows him in India.

शांति और एकता की पुकार

THE CALL TO PEACE & UNITY

the subject of the synod of bishops in 1983 and the subsequent apostolic exhortation bearing the same title from December 2, 1984. In Section 7 of the *promemoria* of 1994 we read: "Inasmuch as Christianity's second millennium is nearing its end, the Church must make itself aware with a revitalized clarity to what extent its faithful have proven faithless in the course of history and sinned against Christ and his gospel."

Referring to efforts in the case of Galileo "to make amends for the injustice done him," the pope asserts: "How could we continue to remain silent about the many forms of cruelty that have been committed even in the name of the faith? Religious wars, Inquisition tribunals, and other instances of infringement on peoples' rights.... It is necessary that the Church as well, in the light of what the Second Vatican Council has said, review on its own initiative the dark pages of its own history and weigh them in the light of the principles of the gospel.... This will in no way do injury to the moral prestige of the Church, which will on the contrary emerge from it strengthened, since it will attest to its honesty and courage in recognizing mistakes committed by its members and, in a certain sense, in its name."

The pope's proposal did not meet with the cardinals' immediate approval. The majority of them were of the opinion that a Christology for the turn of the millennium would be preferable to an ecclesiological emphasis. Among the objections put forth were that any turn-of-the-millennium soul-searching could not ignore the present day; engaging in endless investigations was to be avoided; and finally, recognize that it is impossible to scrutinize the past with modern eyes.

Eastern cardinals feared that any examination of conscience could only justify after the fact much of the former Communist regime's anti-Catholic propaganda. Cardinals from Third World countries expressed little interest in Eurocentric historical quarrels, and worried that an admission of guilt that had nothing to do with their own peoples' culture would have a negative effect on them and be of no benefit at all.

Debate began with a summary of earlier queries presented at the opening of the consistory by secretary of state Cardinal Angelo Sodano:

OPPOSITE, TOP

Religion and theology aside, John Paul II and the Dalai Lama are good friends.

OPPOSITE, CENTER AND BOTTOM

Two kindred souls. John Paul II and Mother Teresa. The Albanian nun was fully the equal of the Polish pope in terms of popularity, charisma, and determination. Also in their missionary zeal, their Eucharistic piety, their views on women, and their opposition to abortion they were spiritual siblings. So it is not surprising that soon after the death of the Nobel Peace Prize–winning nun the process of beatification was begun in Rome and concluded in record time. It is said that as the supreme judge in such affairs, the pope pressured the Curia to work with uncommon speed. On October 19, 2003, only six years after her death, Mother Teresa was beatified in Rome.

"With regard to a comprehensive and universal reappraisal of the past history of the Church, a number of venerable cardinals urge great caution and prudence, since it is an extremely difficult and touchy issue, especially if one hoped to attack it in summary fashion."

The consistory held its discussions behind closed doors, but from statements by the Vatican press spokesman and from comments of individual participants we know that the majority of those present had grave reservations about the proposal. It appears that with the exception of the Curia cardinals Roger Etchegaray and Edward Cassidy, all were either opposed to it or at least highly skeptical. The most vehement objection—and the only one we can study in some detail—was presented by Italian Cardinal Giacomo Biffi, archbishop of Bologna.

In his pastoral letter *Christus Hodie*, Biffi criticized the pope's proposal in a long section titled "Self-Criticism within the Church": "It is a question of considerable importance that must be approached with an equal amount of tact, for it can become a source of uncertainty and accordingly of spiritual insecurity, especially among the simplest and those of least faith.... The Church, if one views it as it truly is, has no sins, for it is the 'whole Christ': its 'head' is the son of God, to whom no moral misconduct can be attributed. Nevertheless, the Church can adopt the feeling of sadness and pain appropriate to the personal misconduct of its members.... They are its sons, yet it does not assume

assume their sins, even when the sins of its children are always deserving of its tears as well as those of the immaculate Virgin. . . . Is it right and proper that we should have to ask for forgiveness for the Church's errors in past centuries? It would be justified if they have been historically proven through investigation that is objective and above all free of antiquated assumptions (which is not always the case). It might also serve to make us appear less uncongenial, and improve our relations with representatives of so-called secular culture, who would welcome our broad-mindedness, though they normally find themselves in no way encouraged to overcome their lack of faith."

The pope made a public response to the cardinals' objections in the apostolic letter *Tertio Millennio Adveniente* (1994): "Hence it is appropriate that, as the Second Millennium of Christianity draws to a close, the Church should become more fully conscious of the sinfulness of her children, recalling all those times in history when they departed from the spirit of Christ and His Gospel and, instead of offering to the world the witness of a life inspired by the values of faith, indulged in ways of thinking and acting that were truly *forms of counter-witness and scandal*.... The Holy Door of the Jubilee of the Year 2000 should be symbolically wider than those of previous Jubilees, because humanity, upon reaching this goal, will leave behind not just a century but a millennium. It is fitting that the Church should make this passage with a clear awareness of what has happened to her during the last ten centuries. She cannot cross the threshold of the new millennium without encouraging her children to purify themselves, through repentance, of past errors and instances of infidelity, inconsistency, and slowness to act. Acknowledging the weakness of the past is an act of honesty and courage that helps us to strengthen our faith, which alerts us to face today's temptations and challenges, and prepares us to meet them."

As these two texts show, the pope accounted for the reservations of Cardinal Biffi, the fiercest opponent of an institutional "mea culpa." He did not speak of failings of the Church, but only of failings of "sons and daughters" of the Church. What seems like a linguistic nicety to protect Church authorities from the suspicion of error has in fact a different background. The pope wanted to adhere to the confession of faith, which the Church describes as "sacred." Here, as in many other of the quoted texts, John Paul II's intention is clear: namely that Church authorities are also "sons and daughters" of the Church, and for that reason share responsibility for the mistakes for which forgiveness is being asked. In the "confession of sin" that

The ember of religion has by no means died out. The pope is firmly convinced that, purified of nationalism and constraint, it can even be rekindled in modern times and serve as a source of light and a guiding principle toward mankind's peaceful coexistence.

In October 1986 John Paul II surprised the world with an unusual invitation: leaders of all the world's religions were to come to Assisi, the city of St. Francis, and pray for peace (pp. 110–11, 113). At the time there were many who failed to see the dramatic urgency of such interfaith exchange. The invitation did not suggest that everyone pray together, but that they come together for prayer in a common place. Even so, there was great agitation within the Church. Self-styled guardians of the "true" faith had no appreciation for such sophistries, and accused the pope not only of religious corruption, but also of blasphemy, betrayal of the First Commandment. How could he set representatives of mythical ancestral cults, adherents of the Buddha, followers of personal and impersonal deities, Zoroastrians, and shamans alongside Jesus of Nazareth, the world's only savior? But John Paul II knew that peace on earth includes, and often enough presupposes, peace between religions. To him it is an outrage that people of faith should wage war against each other and in so doing defile God's testimony on earth. By the time of the second such assembly in Assisi on January 24, 2002, no one complained any longer. On September 11, 2001, Muslim terrorists had shown the whole world how crucial interfaith dialogue really was.

السلام МИР שלום PACE 平和 PEACE शांति
PAIX 和平 PAX FRIEDE ΕΙΡΗΝΗ VREDE PAZ

follows, the pope unabashedly used the term "Church" to recognize misconduct by its sons and daughters, among whose number—as he expressly states—are popes as well as the ordinary faithful: "There can be no privileges for the rich and powerful, and no injustice shall be done to the poor and encumbered.... Does the Church say this insistently enough? Perhaps not. Members of the Church also have their weaknesses. We are the Church, you and I" (Strasbourg, October 8, 1988).

Critics have objected that John Paul II has made too many confessions of sin over the years. Their objection is justified in part, just as it seems fair to argue that many of the pope's activities and sermons lack a degree of moderation: too many trips, too many appeals for peace, declarations in defense of life, appeals to youth, and so on. Yet John Paul II saw himself forced to such confessions by the fact that the Catholic Church only grudgingly accepted his pronouncements.

The soul-searching was entrusted to the most important and largest of the eight commissions coordinated by the Committee for the Great Jubilee, namely the Theological-Historical Commission headed by the Dominican and theologian of the pontifical house, George Cottier. Cottier convened two international colloquiums at the Vatican: one on the roots of Christian Anti-Judaism, which took place from October 30 to November 1, 1997, and a second on the Inquisition, which met a year later, from October 29 to 31, 1998.

Another bit of preparation for the "mea culpa" was a document from the International Theologians Commission titled *The Church and the Faults of the Past*, published in February 2000, which established the theoretical framework for the "Day of Pardon." It was approved by Cardinal Joseph Ratzinger, who, as prefect of the Congregation for the Doctrine of the Faith, consented to the pope's "mea culpa."

These initiatives reduced the pope's isolation in this project, but did not end it altogether. The Curia understood that John Paul II could not be deterred. Self-critical statements in line with the papal intention came in from various national bishops' conferences. By the time the Vatican published its document on the Shoah, *We Remember*, on March 16, 1998, seven bishops' conferences held in various countries had already released similar statements.

Catholic and ecumenical participation in the papal initiative increased over the course of 2000. A review carried out by the Italian journal *Il Regno*, which was published in January 2001 as *Diario del perdono* (*Diary of Forgiveness*), cited twenty-three documents from conferences of Catholic bishops, twenty-five documents from individual bishops, four documents from religious communities (Dominicans, Jesuits, Combonians, and cloistered priests from Rwanda), and two documents from continental bishops' conferences that sided with the pope and his plan for a soul-searching to mark the Jubilee. Of particular interest is that similar initiatives calling for pleas for forgiveness as part of the two-thousand-year celebration of the birth of Christ came from outside the Catholic Church. *Il Regno* names six interdenominational initiatives (Orthodox, Anglican, Presbyterian, Methodist, and Protestant congregations, as well as the Pentecostal movement) and two interreligious ones (with the participation of Buddhists, Muslims, and Baha'is).

The pedagogy of forgiveness introduced by the Polish pope was accepted in the Catholic congregations of Slavic countries as well, which for understandable reasons are more inclined to recall injustices suffered than mistakes committed. Already in 1997, bishops and religious heads of Catholic churches in the East addressed the Orthodox churches with a request for forgiveness "for things our congregations were responsible for over the course of the century." Bohemian bishops followed their example vis-à-vis the Hussites in 1999. Documents from the Polish Synod of 1999 contained a self-critical passage relating to the past. In the year 2000, Croatian Franciscans expressed regret for the participation of their predecessors in the crimes of the Ustachi during World War II. Within the framework of the papal visit to their countries, Cardinal Husar in Lwów, Ukraine, formulated a plea for forgiveness (referring to the entrance of Ukrainian Catholic volunteers into the SS during the German occupation of the country) on June 27, 2001, as did Franjo Komarica, bishop of Bosnia's Banja Luka (referring to World War II and the war in Bosnia) on June 22, 2003.

Through perseverance and by ignoring dissent within his Church, John Paul II succeeded in making the confession of sin—traditionally made by individuals and previously performed in the name of their respective congregations by only a daring few—a common Christian practice at the turn of the new millennium. This success is owed to the strong personality of the man Karol Wojtyla. He has shown the world that he acknowledges his Church's responsibilities as rigorously as he insists on its rights.

What the pope managed to accomplish in Poland—making a major contribution toward greater democracy and justice—would largely be denied him on "the Catholic continent," Central and South America. Unlike the Communists of the Eastern bloc, Latin American rulers did not have a unified view of man; they pretended to be Catholic and friendly toward the Church, but calmly continued their exploitative, repressive policies. Even the pope's spectacular trip to Cuba failed to better conditions for the opposition or relieve the suffering of the poor. This photo shows the pope in Nicaragua in 1983.

Zaire, 1985. The pope appears to be urging people to "stand up for Christ." John Paul II has great hopes for the young, aspiring African Church. Here there is no shortage of priests, and there are no superannuated congregations. Compared to the churches of the north, African congregations tend to be vital and full of enthusiasm. The Church is experiencing tremendous growth in Africa. In many areas, mission stations are centers for charity and medical progress. On the other hand, tribal warfare has again and again sullied the image of Christendom, as did the genocide in Rwanda in 1995, a country composed primarily of Christians.

LA BIENVENUE

"She had heard what people were saying about Jesus, so she came up from behind in the crowd and touched his cloak; for she said to herself, 'If I touch even his clothes, I shall be cured'" (Mark 5:27–28). A photograph from Bangui, in Central Africa, taken in July 1985, recalls this scene from the gospel.

It almost appears as if the enthusiasm of the masses was too much for the pope, but the impression is deceiving. Like no pope before him, John Paul II presents himself as a man, speaks in the first person, avoids the distant "we," and stands firmly behind his message. On the left, an event in Argentina; on the right, another in the capital Buenos Aires, at which he spoke with members of the Polish community.

FOLLOWING SPREAD

John Paul II has visited the Americas a total of twenty-six times. From "secularized" North America he has called for adherence to the Church's moral teachings and greater responsibility for the rest of the world. In Latin America he has reprimanded priests and bishops who subscribed to liberation theology. He does not reject their just concerns—"I, too, am a liberation theologian," he insists; what he does reject is any theological teaching in which he senses the slightest whiff of Marxism. This picture shows the pope in Santa Cruz, Bolivia, in 1988.

nvenido
arija

Even as pope, the onetime goalie has kept his feel for the ball. Also his ready wit. At a meeting of world youth in Toronto, the crowd roared: "John Paul II, we love you." He promptly responded: "The Pope John Paul loves you all." He chooses not to forgo passing through crowds; however, since the assassination attempt in 1981 the "popemobile" has been fitted with bulletproof glass.

John Paul II exerts a great influence on many women. Going on pilgrimage with rosary, songbook, and bare midriff is no contradiction for postmodern youth. Photographed in Coventry, 1982.

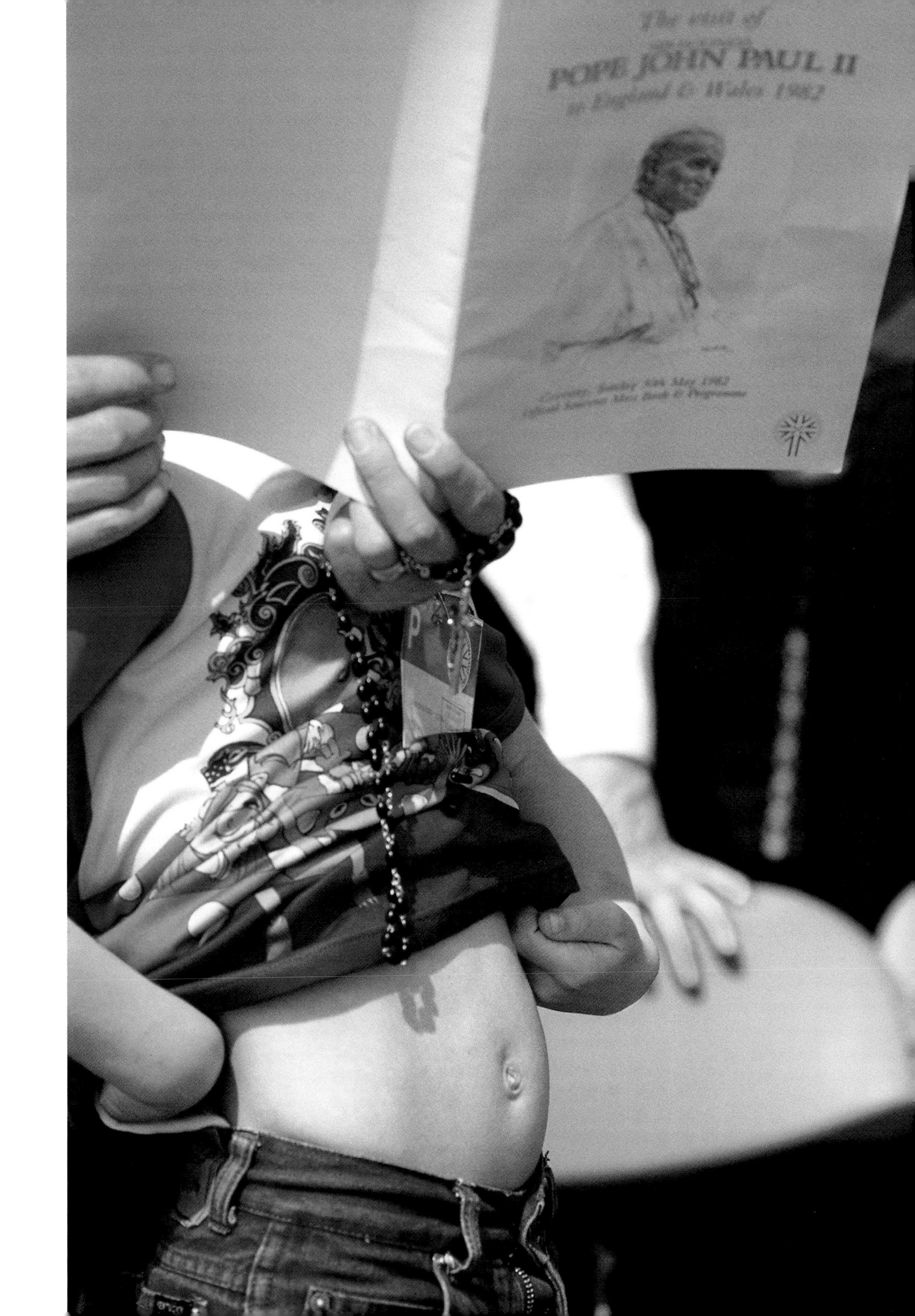
The visit of
POPE JOHN PAUL II
to England & Wales 1982

Avila—home of the Spanish Church teacher and monastic reformer Teresa and the poet and mystic John of the Cross, both of whom exerted a major influence on theology and monastic life in the sixteenth century. It is said that after devouring St. Teresa's autobiography in a single night, Edith Stein immediately had herself baptized. Here, a view of the city walls, which served as the imposing backdrop for a mass in 1982.

TOTUS
TUUS

Psychologists of religion compare the rock cave of the shrine of the Virgin at Lourdes to a sheltering womb. This image shows the pope praying in front of the statue of the Virgin Mary.

Whether the polyglot pontifex prefers listening to march music or jazz is unknown. But it is certain that he is an expert at setting the tempo. Here during a visit to Lusaka, Zambia, in 1989.

OPPOSITE

Looking down on the pope. The stilt-walker will surely not forget this opportunity anytime soon.

ABOVE, TOP

Touching the hem of the pope's robe. The cult of John Paul II began early in his pontificate, and at times takes on magical dimensions.

ABOVE, BOTTOM

For these two infants there are more important things than the pope.

"John Paul, Superstar." No pop group, no soccer player, no politician is capable of provoking such mass excitement. Wherever he goes, people come in droves. In Manila in 1995 some four million people are said to have gathered for the largest mass of all time. On each of his visits to his homeland the pope has attracted ten million of his compatriots. These photographs were taken in Bialystok and Kielce, Poland.

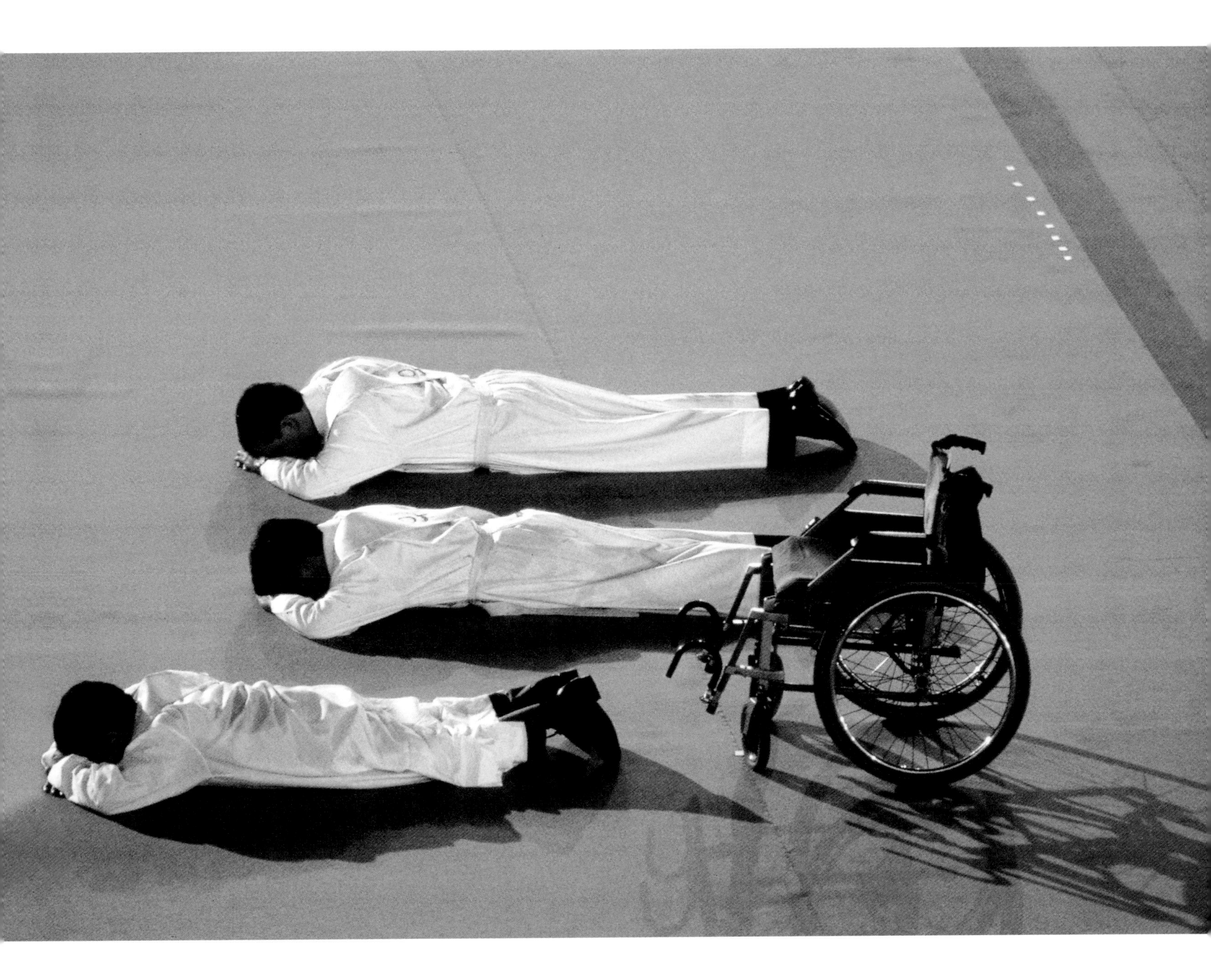

An impressive gesture of humility and respect. On his first arrival in a foreign country, John Paul II always kneels down to kiss the ground. Since walking has become more and more difficult, due to his illness, and he is no longer able to bow down to the ground, he instead has a bowl of soil handed to him. In Palestine this was an eminently political gesture, an implicit demand for the establishment of a sovereign state. The so-called *prostratio* of candidates for the priesthood on their ordination (right) involves another kind of symbolism. They lie on the floor while the names of saints are invoked to intercede for them. Theirs is a gesture of submission meant to indicate that the power they will exercise does not come from themselves.

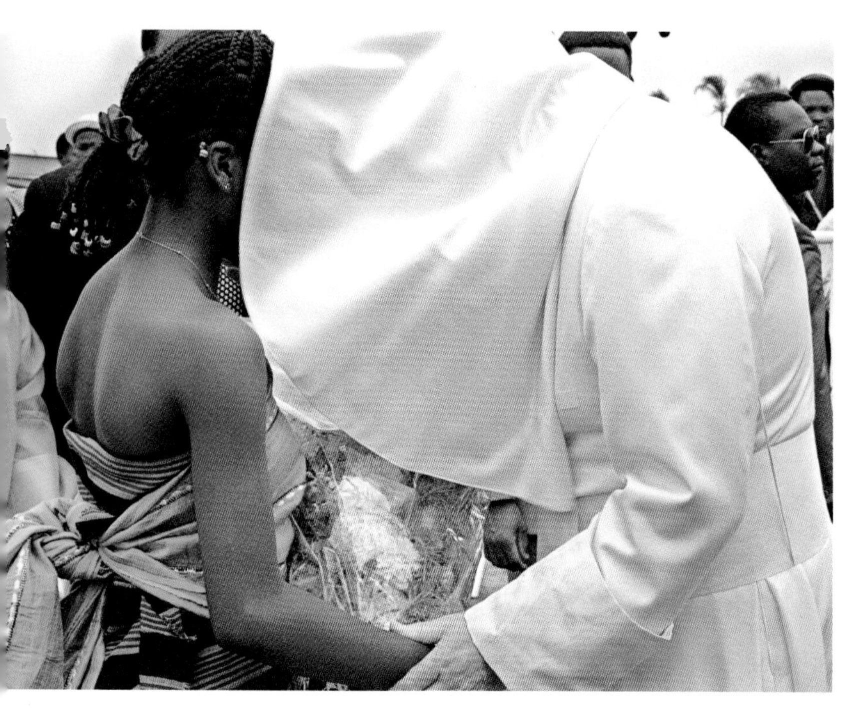

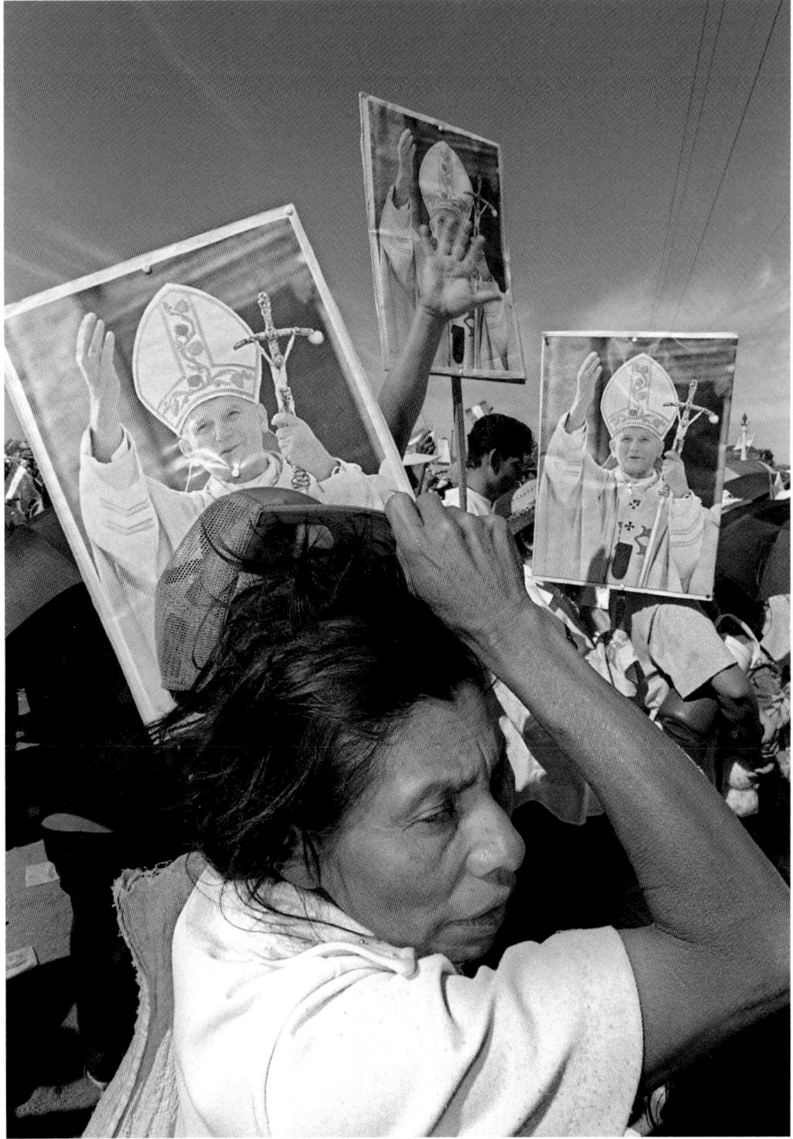

The pope had already assumed the role of global player before the concept of "globalization" had become current. The ceremonial kissing of his hand by an Indian chief, the tête-à-tête with a black beauty arranged by the wind—John Paul II is a pope you can touch, a pope for the people. No wonder that his picture has been printed and sold on millions of balloons, cups, T-shirts, and votive images.

FOLLOWING SPREAD

The public had become used to the notion of a touring pontifex, and his travels were in danger of being ignored by the media. Then in 1998 the pope's travel planners announced a spectacular project: Cuba.

BIENVENIDO
JUAN PABLO II

Hasta la
victoria
siempre

PAGES 145–49

Cuba, the Poland of Central America? Would the pope once again manage to shake a Communist regime to its foundations? Transfixed, observers from around the world followed every word, every step of his journey. Fidel Castro and John Paul II gave each other nothing—even with respect to the length of their speeches. The one railed on about Cuba's social progress, the other, immune to all ideology, hammered away about human rights. It all came together in the streets of Havana (pp. 146–47): Jesus Christ and Che Guevara, the veneration of saints and prostitution. Where else, if not here, is one reminded of the famous statement of the Second Vatican Council: "Nothing human is foreign to the disciples of Christ"?

CAMELLO

¡NO TENGÁIS MIEDO!
JUAN PABLO II

Bienvenido a CUBA
Bienvenido a
de la verdad
y la esperanza

Guest of the pope, the pope as Guest

Whether dictator or democrat, queen or beggar woman, guerilla leader or race-car driver, all gladly pose for a commemorative photograph. Who is missing from these illustrious ranks? The Chinese. There are only a very few governments that consistently refuse to meet with John Paul II. The Central Committee of the Chinese leadership is one of them.

From left to right, top to bottom: Bill Clinton (1999); Queen Elizabeth II (2000); Augusto Pinochet (1987); Fidel Castro (1998); Helmut Kohl (1996); Madeleine Albright (1998); Kurt Waldheim (1998); Mikhail Gorbachev (1996); Lech Walesa (1981); Michael Schumacher (1999); Boris Becker (1986); Brigitte Bardot (1995); Mother Teresa (1997); Tony Blair (2003); Yasir Arafat (1996); Valéry Giscard d'Estaing (1980); Nelson Mandela (1995); George W. Bush (2001).

PUMA.

PREVIOUS SPREAD

The great biblical drama. On his pilgrimage to the Holy Land in the spring of 2000, John Paul II wanted to retrace the route of the faith as described in the Old and New Testaments. From Ur in Chaldea (present-day Iraq), where Abraham heard his calling, by way of Mount Sinai in Egypt, where Moses was presented with the Ten Commandments, to Jerusalem, the site of Christ's crucifixion and resurrection. The political realities did not permit the pope to realize the whole of his itinerary, but he did manage to complete portions of it. This picture shows him on Mount Nebo, in Jordan, where tradition has it that the aged Moses was permitted to look across at the Promised Land (pp. 154–55). In Palestine he visited Bethlehem's Church of the Nativity, in the hall of the Last Supper in Jerusalem he celebrated a mass, and in the Church of the Annunciation in Nazareth he spent a moment in silent prayer (p. 159, bottom). From the Jewish point of view, his visit to Yad Vashem was the high point of this trip. Shaken, his voice breaking, the pope struggled for words—and found none. "Silence," he finally said, for no words were adequate "to lament the appalling tragedy of the Shoah" (p. 159, top).

ABOVE

In Tabgha, the site of the Multiplication of the Loaves near the Sea of Galilee.

Marco Politi

THE BATTLE FOR EUROPE

The naked young woman ran straight toward Karol Wojtyla's "popemobile." She shook her blond mane and seemed determined to leap up onto the pope's car to expose her nude body in protest—protest against the Church's discrimination against women, its rejection of the Pill, its condemnation of divorce and abortion, its ostracism of lesbians and gay men. Police restrained the young woman, but could not prevent a hail of tomatoes from raining down on the papal entourage. Accompanied by then German chancellor Helmut Kohl, John Paul II had envisioned his arrival at the Brandenburg Gate, in the capital of a reunified Germany, somewhat differently. Confronted with the protest signs of homosexuals and other dissenters, Cardinal Joseph Ratzinger, the guardian of Catholic doctrine, affected a frozen smile. The face of Vatican secretary of state Cardinal Angelo Sodano grew dark. Bishop Stanislaw Dziwicz, the pope's private secretary, was the only one who appeared to be unmoved. He knew well that John Paul II would not let himself be influenced by protestors. At the Brandenburg Gate on June 23, 1996, the pope commemorated the historic defeat of National Socialism and Communism and the end to the Cold War. The brown and red dictators, he proclaimed, feared freedom of the spirit above all. In divided Berlin the "cruel face of Communism" had revealed itself for all the world to see. "The closed Brandenburg Gate," he continued, had once "stood there like a symbol of separation," but now has become "a gate to freedom."

Without Karol Wojtyla, the former Soviet leader Mikhail Gorbachev remarked after the collapse of the USSR and the Communist regime in Eastern Europe, these historic events that so radically altered the face of the continent could never have taken place. It is certainly one of the paradoxes of history that a Polish pope, whose country has repeatedly suffered the fate of being divided up among its more powerful neighbors, should have contributed in such a decisive way to the reunification of the very nation that oppressed his countrymen. But European history is full of surprises, and Berlin—a city that in every respect became a symbol of the twentieth century in Europe—was precisely the right place to celebrate the end of an era and the beginning of a new chapter in history.

Karol Wojtyla aspired to be a global pope, and he most certainly is that. But he was profoundly European from the beginning, for in his Polish soul he was always conscious that the fate of his homeland was closely linked to the history of the European continent, and also to its Christian heritage. That day in Berlin with the colorful protest signs was also symbolic of the contradictions of a pontificate that has proclaimed freedom but that has been perceived again and again by opponents within the Church as authoritarian, repressive of open theological debate, and dismissive of many of modern society's demands. Great historical personalities are never one-dimensional. The British cheered Churchill for his victory over Hitler, then dumped him in postwar elections. Karol Wojtyla has always fought for Europe. For its unity, its freedom, and its spirit. His has been a career filled with successes, but not without its defeats as well.

On the eve of the great expansion of the European Union and the acceptance of Poland and other former Warsaw Pact states into its ranks, John Paul II declared in the apostolic exhortation *Ecclesia in Europa* that European unity must become a "new model" of a league of nations, one that bears a great responsibility in the age of globalization.

For a continent torn for centuries by fratricidal warfare and struggles for power, reconciliation is still an indispensable prerequisite to embarking on the road to unity. Karol Wojtyla's own experience of a historic reconciliation lies half a century in the past. The reconciliation in Western Europe achieved between France and Germany by Charles de Gaulle and Konrad Adenauer had its counterpart in Central Europe in the first spectacular gesture of reconciliation between German and Polish bishops during the Second Vatican Council, in which Wojtyla participated as a young man. In fact, he was one of the most vocal champions of such a step. Just imagine: the German Wehrmacht had destroyed his native Poland. A Polish city—Auschwitz—had become the symbol of the extermination of the Jewish people. Millions of Poles had been deported to concentration camps in a systematic attempt to wipe out Poland's national spirit, Poland's culture, and the human dignity of a people condemned by the Third Reich to serve a "master race" as "inferiors." And despite all this, during the Council in 1965 the Polish bishops wrote a letter of reconciliation to the bishops of Germany, the moving final appeal of which read: "We forgive and beg for forgiveness." Among the Polish people—Communists and non-Communists alike—there were many who expressed protest, indignation, incomprehension, and rage over a document that appeared to place the attackers and their victims on the same level. It took not only Christian charity but great vision and civil courage to sign such a letter. Stefan Wyszynski, the primate of Poland, and Karol Wojtyla, archbishop of Kraków, had both.

That letter was the first step in a gradual process of healing the wounds in the relationship between Germans and Poles. Germany's cardinals would remember it in the conclave of 1978. Later, over the course of his pontificate, John Paul II would make having the courage for reconciliation, and recognizing the

OPPOSITE, TOP

In the Yad Vashem memorial with Israeli prime minister Ehud Barak.

OPPOSITE, BOTTOM

In the Church of the Annunciation in Nazareth.

necessity of it, one of the cornerstones of Church policy. He would speak of a "cleansing of memory," and call upon peoples torn by ethnic and religious hatred to perform such an act—in the firm conviction that reconciliation brings with it a constructive dynamic that can set free spiritual and intellectual forces and has consequences that can also bear political, economic, and cultural fruits. Postwar European history, with its reconciliation between historic enemies and its common path toward unification, is a prime example of this.

Bishop Wojtyla's first venture into foreign policy dealt with forgiveness and reconciliation. Fittingly, the first act of his pontificate evoked an almost magical-sounding concept: unity.

Gniezno, June 3, 1979, a Sunday: a huge crowd of people welcomed the pope in the ancient capital of the Polish kings. Twenty-four hours earlier, John Paul II had embarked on his triumphal tour of Poland. Millions of people lined his route, crosses taking the place of red flags, which had suddenly disappeared. Karol Wojtyla strode through the crowds like a monarch. The whole world watched as the pope of Rome challenged the Soviet empire—in a country that had always conceived itself to be a bulwark of Catholicism against the "enemy in the East." In foreign ministries there was fear that the world's political situation would be destabilized, even though it was felt that the influence of this pope was still primarily on the Poles. But John Paul II by no means had in mind only the fate of his homeland. "Is it not the will of the Holy Ghost," he called out on the huge square in front of Gniezno's cathedral, "that this Polish pope, this Slavic pope, should at this very time make visible the spiritual unity of Christian Europe?... Perhaps God chose him so that he might bring to the community of the Church an understanding for words and languages that still sound foreign to ears accustomed to German, Anglo-Saxon, and French sounds."

There, in a place the vast majority of Europeans had never heard of, the pope showed himself to be a political leader with vision. But this was not something visionary, it was simply an intuitive perception of a possible turn in history. Can a mystic change into a politician? The example of Karol Wojtyla shows that it is possible. Wojtyla is by constitution a profoundly mystical man. You only need to watch him when he prays. When the pope kneels down to pray—preferably before the image of the Virgin, to whom he often gives the title "queen" of whatever country he happens to be visiting—you can see how he plumbs the depths of his soul. To him prayer is a complete, one could almost say passionate, surrender into the arms of his God. During this journey into another dimension his face is transformed, it loses its fleshiness, its texture and color. It is these mystical roots that give rise to his deep conviction of the dignity of man. For Wojtyla, man is not only the image of God, as the Bible teaches, but also *gloria Dei*, the glory of God. For that reason human dignity must be preserved under all circumstances.

A major discord occurred at an interfaith meeting with Jewish and Muslim religious leaders in Jerusalem. Grand Mufti Ikrima Sabri, Islam's highest representative in the Holy City, declined to participate in the meeting and sent a subordinate, Sheik Tazis al Tamimi. In a heated speech, Tazis accused the Jewish "occupiers" of genocide against the Palestinians and reaffirmed the Muslims' sole claim to Jerusalem, then left the meeting in a huff.

"Operation Old Friend"—the code name used by Israeli security forces for the papal visit.

This fundamental conviction is a constant thread running through the pope's political engagement—from Poland in the 1970s to the globalized world in the new millennium.

In this scenario a key role falls to Europe. As a young bishop, Wojtyla shied away from politics, preferring philosophy instead. It was his friends in Kraków, Catholic intellectuals associated with the Znak publishing house and the weekly *Tygodnik Powszechny*, who urged him to take a stand on social and political questions. His tenure as a cardinal in Kraków during the 1970s was his apprenticeship. On the throne of St. Peter during the ceremonial mass on the inauguration of his pontificate, Wojtyla showed who he was when he extended his crosier with its cross toward the crowd and with expansive gestures gave his benediction to thousands of exhilarated men and women. John Paul II has ended up dealing in politics with the confidence of a chess player who moves his figures with patience and clarity of mind.

A few years before John Paul II made his extraordinary trip to Poland in 1979, the conference on security and cooperation in Europe had taken place in Yalta. All the countries of the old continent, including Soviet Russia, and the United States and Canada had signed a treaty of peaceful coexistence. In the European states separated by the Iron Curtain, there began a process of dialogue, rapprochement, and increased (though still limited and controlled) exchange of people and ideas. Yet the boundaries established at the Yalta conference remained untouched. Under the pretext of religious exhortation, John Paul II spoke in Gniezno of going beyond Yalta, and conjured up a vision of a Europe in which individual peoples not only live together but unite as one. To the ossified *apparatchiks* in the East, who clung to the mantra of "dual systems," the Polish pope (the Slavic pope, as he proudly emphasizes) extended the remarkable image of "spiritual unity" for the Continent. With this he triggered a movement—at that time scarcely imaginable—that would perforate the Iron Curtain and ultimately tear it down altogether.

In foreign policy, John Paul II has never been a rigid ideologue. As a bishop he never dreamed of an end to the Communist regime in Poland, and as a newly elected pope he did not argue for an end to Moscow's Communist empire. After 1989 he did not call for the breakup of the Soviet Union (except for his demand for freedom for the three Baltic states). He did, however, raise his political voice on every available occasion. Beginning in the 1980s he persistently argued for breaking the taboo of Yalta and awakening in the European public a sense of the deep unity of the Continent. And the more the Kremlin emphasized the untouchability of borders and the differences between systems, the more emphatically the pope stressed the indestructible relationship between the Eastern European nations and those of the West—a brotherhood of the heart, of thought, of faith, of culture. Naming the Slavic St. Cyril and St. Methodius as European patrons alongside St. Benedict was more a political demonstration than a religious act. It was neither the first time nor the last that John Paul II would make use of symbols to change history.

Wojtyla's relentless insistence that the Church must embrace both Eastern and Western traditions, and his constant emphasis on the fact that he is a "Slavic pope," was not motivated by any nationalistic ambition, but was part of a cultural plan for the unification of a Europe torn apart by World War II. That it was even more a political program would become evident later.

And the pope's persistence paid off. With the fall of the Berlin Wall and the collapse of the Soviet empire, a number of John Paul II's hopes were realized—but not all of them. His dream that the East might bring to the consumption-oriented West the light of a stronger spirituality, a religious renewal, and moral regeneration, remained unfulfilled. After the fall of the wall, John Paul II did not encounter in the liberated countries the likes of Aleksandr Solzhenitsyn, who cried out for honesty and morality. The pope had to recognize that in the countries released from Soviet rule a predatory brand of capitalism was spreading on a scale that horrified him. The small peep-show shed that stood for a time on Plac Trzech Krzyzy (Three Crosses Square) in Warsaw became a distorted symbol of the hopes for moral rebirth in Poland and the other Eastern European countries John Paul II had nourished. This he had not envisioned, for on his first trip to Poland as pope the young people had cheered him while holding aloft wooden crosses. After the fall of the wall an unbridled, primitive nationalism also came to the fore that in some countries led to cruel ethnic conflict. That was not what John Paul II was thinking of when he preached the freedom of peoples from Soviet repression. "The end of Yalta," he confided in those years to the Italian Catholic philosopher Rocco Buttiglione, "must not lead to a situation like the one that arose after Versailles"—in other words, not to nationalistic blindness. "A patriot," the pope assured his confidant, "loves his fatherland and has respect for the fatherlands of others. A nationalist wishes to subjugate the other's fatherland." This is precisely what happened in many of the states of Eastern Europe following the end of Soviet rule, especially on the Balkan peninsula, where Tito's Yugoslavia was falling apart. "Sarajevo is the city where it all started...," the aging and already ailing pontiff prophetically lamented to the journalists who accompanied him on his summer vacation in the Val d'Aosta. To someone whose father had served in a Habsburg regiment—at a time when Galicia was still part of Emperor Franz Joseph's Danubian monarchy—the ominous name Sarajevo stood for the outbreak of World War I.

In the hectic and convoluted process that led to the breakup of Yugoslavia, the Vatican bears a great

Meeting with Yasir Arafat in Bethlehem.

responsibility. John Paul II managed to persuade the powerful Croatian lobby to be among the first to recognize the independence of Croatia and Slovenia, and thereby exclude any other possible union of the states of the Yugoslav federation. Soon the world witnessed the merciless duel between the dictators Slobodan Milosevic and Franjo Tudjman, both ruthless ex-Communists with bloodthirsty militias under their control. The sole distinction between them was that the Croat nationalist Tudjman jumped onto the right side in time—that of the West. Although he was in no way inferior to his counterpart in Belgrade in his contempt for democracy and ethnic minorities, he was tolerated, if not admired, as a dictator, and thus able to end his days in peace and quiet. With ethnic war raging in the Balkans, which soon ravaged the territory of Bosnia with monstrous vehemence, John Paul II did not fall into the trap of those Orthodox Serbs and Croatian Catholics who claimed to be fighting in the name of Christianity against the advance of Islam onto the Balkan peninsula. On the contrary, the long war in the former Yugoslavia gave the pope a chance to take a decisive stand against the theory of "cultural wars." The Catholic pope defended the rights of Muslim Bosnia. In view of the bloody war, he felt it his duty and moral responsibility, despite evident danger to life and limb (on April 12, 1997, a strong explosive was discovered under a bridge that the pope and his entourage were to cross) to travel to Sarajevo. But that was not all. During the long years of the siege of Sarajevo he evolved a new theory of humanitarian intervention. "When I see someone attacked on the street," he explained, "I have to become involved and disarm the attacker." Thus the good Samaritan is not only required to heal wounds, but to stop them from being inflicted.

His words are a challenge to Europe to resist the seductions of nationalism, to avoid disputes between cultures, and to be prepared to intervene and mitigate conflicts. Here again he had in mind the deeper meaning of reconciliation, which had motivated him back during the Second Vatican Council to argue for easing the tensions between Germany and Poland. In a speech he prepared for a visit to Sarajevo in 1994—the trip was ultimately postponed and the speech never delivered—John Paul II called on Catholics, Orthodox Christians, and Muslims to take up the challenge of forgiveness and reconciliation: "One must ask for forgiveness and be able to forgive." In this sense, recent history in Europe must point the way.

Despite all the attentiveness and goodwill with which the Polish pope follows the European process of unification, because of his views he has again and again found himself in conflict with cultural changes across the Continent. Repeatedly, John Paul II has opposed the policies of the European Parliament, which supports marriage-like cohabitation and other rights for homosexuals. The issues of abortion and euthanasia have even brought him into conflict with the basic tenets of parliamentary democracy. Equating the destruction of a fertilized ovum with murder, and abortion with the Holocaust, he triggered violent controversy. His harsh words were unacceptable to numbers of Christians and non-Christians. In the encyclical *Evangelium Vitae* of 1995 we read: "When a parliamentary or public majority... upholds the legitimacy of... killing unborn human life, is this not perhaps a tyrannical sentence against the weakest and most defenseless of human creatures?"

The fate of present-day Europe matters to Karol Wojtyla, however much he is troubled by certain developments; in those developments he sees the specter of an "anti-Christian program" that began with the Enlightenment and has brought us to a ubiquitous "culture of death." The Vatican's theologians have branded the so-called morning-after pill as murder, and condemned the entire twentieth century as an age of annihilation. John Paul II is fearful of being forced to watch the European continent, a foundation pillar of Christianity, abandon the traditional religion of its forebears. At the first special session of the European Synod of Bishops in 1991 there was open discussion of the "apostasy of the masses," the nightmare of millions of men and women quietly turning their backs on the Catholic Church. Churches are emptying, the number of priests is in constant decline, confessionals are empty, attendance at Sunday mass is increasingly sparse. Traditional piety is changing into a dubious homemade faith, a do-it-yourself religion in which the old norms, dogma, and precepts are being abandoned and relativized.

In the twenty-five years of this pontificate, the appearance of the Catholic Church has distinctly changed. The number of the faithful has risen from 756 million in 1978 to 1.6 billion. In the Americas alone the number of Catholics has risen by 160 million, and now stands at 528 million. In Asia their number has risen from 63 million to 108 million. The greatest growth has been in Africa, with an increase from 54 million to 135 million Catholic Christians. In Europe, however, the number of Catholics is stagnating, though this is due in part to Europe's slowing population growth rate. When Karol Wojtyla was elected pope, a third of the population of Europe was Catholic, and since then the percentage has dropped to 26 percent.

The numbers for underdeveloped countries are no cause for rejoicing for the Church. In the traditionally heavily Catholic nations of Latin America, such as Brazil and the Central American countries, radical Protestant sects are aggressively missionizing. And in Africa, Christianity finds itself facing a no less aggressive Islam. In Africa, which Pope John Paul II refers to as the "continent of hope," the number of converts to Islam is rising faster than the number of new Christians. At any rate, the underdeveloped countries cannot be used

FOLLOWING SPREAD
At the Wailing Wall in March 2000.

On December 24, 1999, Pope John Paul II proclaimed the beginning of a Holy Year for the Church. The Holy Doors in St. Peter's and St. Paul's Outside the Walls would remain open until January 6, 2001. In this jubilee year the Church hoped for cleansing and reawakening. Ecumenically, the year began promisingly enough. Orthodox, Anglican, and Lutheran leaders knelt with the pope in harmony on the threshold of the Holy Door of St. Paul's Outside the Walls. On March 22 the pope, together with the highest-ranking cardinals, made a confession of guilt that was widely reported. In August a million young people once again made a pilgrimage to Rome for World Youth Day. But then public perception of the jubilee clouded. The declaration *Dominus Jesus*, issued by the Congregation for the Doctrine of the Faith, reaffirmed the Catholic Church's sole legitimacy, causing a certain strain in ecumenical relations. The beatification of Pope Pius IX brought a chill into Church relations with Jews. To many, Catholicism appeared to be on a backward course. Nonetheless, one should not discount the symbolic significance and the "spiritual fruits" of the Holy Year. That the pope had the greatness to admit mistakes placed the existential drama of guilt and forgiveness before the eyes of the whole world. The profound earnestness reflected in such ceremonies gave even nonbelievers and agnostics a perception of religious awe.

OPPOSITE

Reading the message for World Peace Day and New Year's greetings at the turn of the millennium.

FOLLOWING SPREAD

Children's jubilee. Boys and girls from around the world at a Holy Year celebration on St. Peter's Square on January 2, 2000.

as consolation for failures in the developed nations. The Roman Church historian Pietro Scoppola has remarked, "If the Catholic Church does not succeed in preserving its vitality and attractiveness in the developed countries, it will one day be faced with the same problems in the underdeveloped ones—namely when those countries have attained the same level of modernization and secularization that we now know."

The crisis in the Catholic Church in Europe can be seen from the meager numbers of diocesan priests. Their number decreased from 149,903 in 1996 to 144,215 in 2001; consecrations were down from 2,600 to 2,250. In the same period, the number of nuns in Europe, somewhat the foot soldiers and auxiliary troops of the Catholic Church, sank from 396,898 to 357,840. These figures are taken from the Holy See's statistical annual. Wojtyla is fighting for the soul of Europe, but he has little influence over the younger generations, due to his demonization of birth control, his obsessive battle against abortion, his rigorous rejection of divorce (a position shared by no other Christian confession), and his categorical "no" to the admission of women to the priesthood. He has had all these positions reinforced again and again by the prefect of the Congregation for the Doctrine of the Faith, Cardinal Joseph Ratzinger. When the pope insists that the union of two people of the same sex is "a regrettable distortion of what love and matrimony between man and woman is meant to be," he meets with incomprehension on the part of a large number of younger people and many not so young. It was no coincidence that among the 300,000 participants in the parade of gay men and lesbians staged in Rome on July 8 in the Jubilee year 2000, half were heterosexuals; men and women, often even families with children. They marched to the Colosseum to protest the Vatican's attempt to forbid the demonstration. In the area of stringent prohibitions, the faithful do not go along with Karol Wojtyla. In parishes, a large majority of priests who sit in confessionals feel closer to ordinary believers than to the Vatican, with its draconian judgments; many bishops are embarrassed by this, though they choose not to voice their dissent officially. The priest and psychoanalyst Eugen Drewermann argues that Jesus of Nazareth stood for man's healing liberation, not his subjection to an institution that judges and condemns. According to Drewermann, whose teachings have been denounced by Church authorities and who has been suspended as a priest, too many people no longer know how to deal with the pope's stern pronouncements, his expansion of intermediary authority, his fixation on issues of sexual morality, his dogmatic formulations and endless catechizing.

That is the flip side of the Wojtyla phenomenon. This is a man who holds the masses spellbound as a pilgrim of the faith and witness to hope, but who meets with antagonism when seen as an authoritarian ruler.

Secular Europe can only reject the stream of bans issuing from Rome. And millions of Catholic men and women can only refuse to accept the notion of parliamentary delegates manipulated from afar, obedient to "doctrinal" directives put out by the Holy See, which outline the most recent Vatican guidelines on how Catholic politicians are to behave. If there have been no spectacular public protests against Wojtyla's positions in recent years, it is only because people have already quietly disassociated themselves from them in their own consciences. The uprising of the "We Are the Church" movement in Austria following the scandal relating to the Viennese cardinal Hans Hermann Groer, accused of numerous homosexual liaisons while a priest, was only the tip of the iceberg of unease and dissent. Ultimately Groer was forced to resign his position as archbishop of Vienna. The movement expressed the demand for a more democratic Catholicism, criticizing the fact that the faithful have no say in the important decisions of the Church, especially the election of bishops.

Moreover, many bishops find it difficult to accept in every case the Roman Curia's "no," expressed by order of the pope. Cardinal Karl Lehmann, chairman of the conference of German bishops, has repeatedly tried to nudge the Vatican toward a more humane stance regarding believers who have divorced and remarried, yet the pope denies them Communion. In the eyes of those close to the pontiff, his insistence has cast him in a poor light. For years Lehmann was refused elevation to cardinal, though the German episcopate had expressed its confidence in him by electing him to four terms as chairman. The Vatican was unbending; opposing the pope has its price. Then in the consistory of 2001 an unusual situation arose. A week after the publication of a list of candidates for cardinal, John Paul II circulated a kind of postscript: a second list on which Karl Lehmann was included after all. For John Paul II to take such a step required the protestations of cardinals like the Vatican's top diplomat, Roger Etchegaray. Even the secretary of state, Cardinal Angelo Sodano, had to intervene.

Since the second special session of the European Synod of Bishops in October 1999, the fronts have already cleared somewhat. Cardinal Carlo Maria Martini, then archbishop of Milan (now retired and living in Jerusalem), proposed a reform agenda for the third millennium: he called for "new and more far-reaching forms of collegiality" and the convocation of a new council to take up unresolved issues such as the dearth of priests, the role of women in the Church, the participation of the laity in Church life, confession, sexuality, the institution of marriage, and relations with Orthodox Christians.

Although Martini is highly respected by other Christian churches, John Paul II let it be known through his confidants that Martini's suggestions had not evoked serious discussion. Regarding the Italian cardinal's call for new forms of collegiality (the participation of bishops in the government of the Church), Lublin's Bishop Josef Zycinski explained to the press with some irony: "The notion that new Church structures could solve the problems at issue derives not so much from theological considerations as from some kind of magical wishful thinking."

Nevertheless, despite dismissal from the top, the agenda is to be discussed at the next conclave.

Unconcerned with differences of opinion within the Church regarding modern society, Karol Wojtyla is not letting up in his battle for Europe. As head of the Church he nurtures the desire that the peoples of the Continent preserve the spiritual heritage of Christianity, and that reference to its "Christian roots" be firmly stated in any future European constitution. As a political leader, he is convinced that a united Europe has a role to play on the world stage.

I recall a flight with the pope from Rome to Mexico City in January 1999. Below us lay the vast expanse of the Atlantic Ocean. Propped on his cane, John Paul II came up to us journalists to take our questions. We brought up the world's political situation. I was sitting next to him, and could study his distinctive features. He had bowed his head slightly as if quietly meditating, not looking at anyone. "Since the collapse of the Soviet Union, the United States is the only power left.... I do not know whether that is good or not. But that is how it is." The only one. A superpower without rivals. Thinking back to his first trip to Mexico in 1979, he added pensively: "When I came here the first time, there was a confrontation between East and West, between the United States and the Eastern bloc. Today there is no longer any such conflict." "And how is the world affected by that, Holy Father?" I asked. With the hint of irony that is so typical of him in intimate circles, he replied: "Ah, let us drop the subject...!"

In Karol Wojtyla's geopolitical thinking, Europe should take its place on a world stage now dominated by an all-too-solitary empire. "God bless America," he once said when stepping onto U.S. soil. The American people's religious faith and love of freedom are dear to him; however, his view of the world is a multipolar one. He is deeply convinced that the world's peoples and cultures must work together for the progress of the entire "human family," resolving crises and dealing with problems together. He finds unilateral decisions repugnant, hegemonic ambitions suspect.

Pope Wojtyla argues for an open Europe that puts solidarity into practice and works for world peace. He insists that Europe must be synonymous with openness. In his exhortation *Ecclesia in Europa* of June 28, 2003, he assigns a specific task to the peoples of the European continent: Europe must "erect a new model of unity in diversity, a community of reconciled nations open to the other continents and involved in the ongoing process of globalization."

This is a precise plan, and although the pope tirelessly calls upon us to recall the Continent's

Excited children, laughing bishops, and a fluttering white dove: Children's Day at the Vatican, the kind of celebration the pope delights in; 30,000 boys and girls pray and picnic on St. Peter's Square.

Christian roots, European values can also be understood in a secular sense as the affirmation of the dignity of the individual, of the value of reason, freedom, and democracy, of the constitutional state and the separation of politics and religion. Karol Wojtyla is not incorrect when he says that at the very moment when it is solidifying and expanding its economic and political union, Europe is experiencing a profound crisis in values and a serious lack of political engagement. The European Union will not survive, he insists, if it is nothing but a geographical and economic construct. In this John Paul II echoes the thinking of any number of European intellectuals. Europe is much more than a mere patchwork of geography; it is above all a cultural and historical concept. Translated into political terminology, this means that Europe can be an important factor in global politics if it succeeds in presenting its own notion of international relationships and its own social and economic order. This is no trivial task.

In his speeches and writings, John Paul II has contributed several building blocks to this new European structure. For years he has continued to brood over something that surfaced toward the end of the Communist regime in Eastern Europe. It is his determined campaign against what he calls predatory capitalism. Twenty-four hours before his appearance at the Brandenburg Gate on a trip to Germany in 1996, John Paul II drew some conclusions about the great change: "Dear sisters, dear brothers," he invoked in Paderborn before some 80,000 people who had gathered on a summer meadow beneath a cloudy sky, "we must not allow a world to emerge that is again stamped by radical capitalist ideology." Several years before, on a visit to Riga, the capital of the former Soviet republic of Latvia, he had already expressed his fear of a society that is oriented solely toward material considerations and that excludes its weakest members. At that time he caused something of a stir by lending present-day validity to the fears of Karl Marx, the founding father of socialism: "The exploitation to which an inhuman capitalism subjected the proletariat was an evil condemned by the social doctrine of the Church," he proclaimed before a somewhat astonished Latvian audience, "and this was essentially the seed

Praying hands and the Last Judgment. More and more, the pope speaks of age and death: "Pray for me!"

of truth in Marxism." In Paderborn he emphatically proclaimed his moral mission: "A radical individualism that ultimately destroys society must not be allowed to prevail."

The model Europe, he explains in *Ecclesia in Europa*, must attack the pressing problems of poverty and unemployment; it must recognize that the individual is valuable for his own sake, and that work represents a good that all of society must embrace. No less grave is its responsibility for the proper use of the world's resources. John Paul II echoes the concerns of ecologists in his condemnation of specific developments: "In many regions man…has destroyed forests and land areas, made the air unbearable to breathe, upset the hydrogeological and atmospheric balance, and exposed vast stretches to the advance of desert." In this connection he again denounces abortion and genetic interferences, which "are indisputably linked to the killing of human embryos." Especially on the level of global politics, Europe, according to Wojtyla's vision, has a historic task to fulfill. A unified Europe must actively cooperate in globalization, and in its international relationships assert the principles of equality, justice, and freedom. "The market," the pope resolutely insists, "requires that it be controlled by social forces and by the state in such a manner as to guarantee that the basic needs of the entire society are satisfied." A further demand, which derives from Wojtyla's reflections on the tragedies of the recent past, is the obligation "to work tirelessly for the building of peace within the boundaries of Europe and throughout the world." He places the problem of mass migration in this context. "Openness" and "acceptance" are terms that appear again and again in his apostolic writings devoted to Europe. The new Europe, he asserts, must not be an enclosure, but an "open and hospitable continent," one called upon to create an attitude of "acceptance and welcome" toward immigrants, and thereby create a resource for the European future. Given the flare-up of xenophobia in various European countries—in Great Britain as well as France, Spain, Italy, Germany, and Austria—Wojtyla is asking a great deal. Europe must become a common home "into which everyone is accepted, in which no one is discriminated against, and all are treated as members of one great family." Every immigrant, the pope insists, has the right to be incorporated into the social and cultural structure of his new nation. His basic rights must be honored. Alongside its lofty ideals, the papal program also includes a pragmatic approach to the problem of immigration: "State authorities are responsible for controlling the stream of immigration…admission must always be accomplished in accordance with law, and therefore, when necessary, proceed to eliminate violations." Ultimately, the way Europe deals with the issue of migration will be a standard by which the quality of that society will be measured.

Opening the Holy Door.

While John Paul II demands that we recall Europe's Christian roots, he also acknowledges the many cultural strains that have impacted the Continent's physiognomy: Rome and ancient Greece, the Celts and the Germans, the Slavs and the Finno-Ugric peoples, and the contributions made by Jewish and Islamic cultures. There comes a moment, however, when all geopolitical visions must face a trial by fire. Karol Wojtyla's was the Iraq conflict of 2003.

When Cardinal Pio Laghi left the West Wing of the White House after a meeting with President George W. Bush on March 2, 2003, he had the distinct feeling that all was lost. Nothing and no one would prevent the United States from attacking Iraq. The eighty-one-year-old cardinal could not know, of course, that—as was recently confirmed by a secret Pentagon report—the American president had already subscribed to plans for a war in Iraq on August 29, 2002. But as the Vatican's former ambassador to the United States from 1980 to 1990 under Presidents Reagan and Bush Sr., with whom he is personally acquainted, Laghi had enough insight into the decision-making mechanisms in Washington to know where there was room for negotiation and where there was not. And during his altogether friendly, though quite formal, meeting—the two exchanged long monologues—George W. Bush made it abundantly clear that he was not prepared for a change of course. Moreover, just before he received John Paul II's special envoy, the president had held a war council with his top military men in the situation room of the White House, discussing the specifics of air attacks with General Tommy Franks. An unmistakable signal. The papal message that Laghi had delivered was pointless. Pointless were the cardinal's aggrieved words: "The Holy Father is terribly, terribly, terribly concerned." Pointless also was Wojtyla's urgent appeal to Bush in his letter: "I assure you, Mr. President, that I am praying for you and for America, and that in my prayers I beg the Lord to strengthen you in the search for peace."

As a good Christian, Cardinal Laghi quoted the old dictum *spes contra spem*—hope against all hopelessness. But he knew that the game was over. He had not failed to notice that on the eve of his meeting with Bush, White House spokesman Ari Fleischer had vehemently declared that the president would not have "conditions dictated to him" by the pope. It was not the first time that officials in Washington had treated John Paul II like a disturbance to the peace. Bush's influential advisor Condoleezza Rice had openly rejected the pope's insistence that war must be prevented through negotiation: "I do not understand this position," she haughtily explained. "I do not understand how a person can consider it immoral to try to prevent the deaths of tens of thousands, hundreds of thousands, even possibly millions of

Kneeling at the threshold of the Holy Door.

people by proceeding against a brutal regime that has used chemical weapons against its own people and against its neighbors." To the Vatican this showed a distressing want of diplomatic tact.

Nevertheless, the pope insisted on dispatching a personal emissary to remind Bush, with the full weight of his moral authority and worldwide respect, that "any decision about the use of force must be made within the framework of the United Nations." Pio Laghi, who was denied a meeting with reporters in the White House, later explained at Washington's National Press Club that Pope John Paul II had pointed out the grave dangers in the event of a war against Iraq. Cardinal Laghi spoke of the suffering of the Iraqi people and the suffering of those involved in military operations. He also pointed out the danger of a break between Islam and Christianity, and once again stressed publicly the pope's profound conviction that a unilateral war against Iraq was unjust and immoral.

Cardinal Laghi's mission to Washington was the last card John Paul II played in an attempt to prevent an invasion of Iraq.

To the aging pope, this war was extraordinary in that it affected the entire world and the course of history in the century just begun. John Paul II had always been against war. To some extent that is part of his job. He was against the Gulf War of 1991, he was against the war in Kosovo in 1998, and against the war in Afghanistan in 2001. But never had he orchestrated such a flurry of diplomatic, media, and religious activities as he did to oppose the war George W. Bush wished to wage on Iraq. And it had nothing to do with pacifism.

A Polish pope cannot be a pacifist. Any Polish patriot carries in his blood, as it were, the history of his own country, one that has been attacked, divided, and wiped off the map. From childhood, Poles are taught to keep alive the memory of the nation's struggles against tyranny and to cherish the names of those who rose up in arms against attack. John Paul II has himself reminded us in several of his speeches that there are times when war is necessary. What terrified the pope about the aggressive, unilateral policy of the ideologues who swarm around Bush was the affront to international law, a refusal to accept a global equilibrium based on the universally recognized structure of the United Nations, however imperfect and in need of reform that organization may be. No nation or group of nations can play

"From the beginning of my Pontificate, my thoughts had been on this Holy Year 2000 as an important appointment. I thought of its celebration as a providential opportunity during which the Church, thirty-five years after the Second Vatican Council, would examine how far she had renewed herself, in order to be able to take up her evangelizing mission with fresh enthusiasm. Has the Jubilee succeeded in this aim? Our commitment, with its generous efforts and inevitable failings, is under God's scrutiny."

FROM THE APOSTOLIC LETTER *NOVO MILLENNIO INEUNTE*.

IOANNES PAVLVS II P M
PORTAM SANCTAM
ANNO IVBILAEI MCMLXXV
A PAVLO PP VI
RESERATAM ET CLAVSAM
APERVIT ET CLAVSIT
ANNO IVB HVMANAE REDEMP
MCMLXXXIII MCMLXXXIV
PAVLVS VI PONT MAX
HVIVS PATRIARCALIS
VATICANAE BASILICAE
PORTAM SANCTAM
APERVIT ET CLAVSIT
ANNO IVBILAEI MCMLXXV
PORTA SANCTA

God. John Paul II is adamant about this. The problem of peace cannot be considered without regard to moral principles. Politics, he asserts, "are subject to moral judgment." On a global scale, they require a legal framework for stopping wars and the violence born of the evil residing in the human psyche.

In his meetings in the dramatic months before the war with some of the protagonists of the great political struggle—U.N. secretary-general Kofi Annan, Spanish prime minister José Maria Aznar, Iraqi foreign minister Tariq Aziz, British prime minister Tony Blair, the vice president of the Iranian parliamentary Sayyed Mohammad Khatami, German foreign minister Joschka Fischer, and Italian prime minister Silvio Berlusconi—the pope repeated again and again his deep conviction: the United Nations and only the United Nations can guarantee international justice. Woe be to anyone who believes that a world without law would be a better one. An open international body, on the other hand, can serve to further the cause of human rights, freedom, and peace. Karol Wojtyla spoke in the spirit of a Europe that has freed itself from the bloody burden of the past. As a Pole and as a European, he has had a taste of the kind of war that has soaked the soil of Europe with blood for centuries, and he has reflected deeply on his experience. Power wars, religious wars, wars of expansion, ideological, economic, and ethnic wars, wars fomented by totalitarian systems, and wars declared by democratic regimes. The official rationale of a war—the establishment of "sacred boundaries," defense of the "true faith," the acquisition of *Lebensraum*, expansion of a "culture"—has virtually always been a lie. Like the great men and women who had learned from the horrors of a world war illumined by the glow of crematorium ovens, Karol Wojtyla set out on a path of reconciliation and followed it to its conclusion. It was the same path that was traversed in the postwar period by people such as Robert Schuman, Jean Monnet, Konrad Adenauer, and Alcide De Gasperi in their creation of the European Community. With absolute consistency, from the fall of 2002 until the outbreak of war in March 2003, the Holy See sought to strengthen through diplomacy the unexpected triple alliance among France, Germany, and Russia, which within the framework of the Security Council of the United Nations opposed blanket authorization of a military attack. Frocked diplomats discreetly saw to it that Mexico and Chile, the two Latin American countries with seats in the Security Council, refused to support the British-American resolution. In this way Washington was prevented from achieving the necessary majority for attack on Iraq under a U.N. mandate.

The door is closed, the Holy Year 2000 is history. It did not make history as did the Second Vatican Council. But again and again it allowed us to see the inner strength of Christendom, provided hopeful signs, and stimulated renewal through unprecedented self-criticism.

The pope made a conscious effort to lend a voice to the overwhelming majority of Europeans who opposed the war. Not only in France and Germany, but also in countries like Italy, Great Britain, Spain, and Poland, whose political leaders stood behind the United States, the majority of the public was against the war.

As pope—much like his medieval predecessors—Karol Wojtyla has always viewed with suspicion the notion of a single, all-powerful world ruler. As a European he is a multilateralist as a matter of course. As a man of faith, finally, he deplores all political messianism. He rejects the notion that any nation should pose as representative of the good in the struggle against evil. The Jesuit director of Radio Vatican, Pasquale Borgomeo, has said that no one can presume "to play the role of accuser, witness for the prosecution, judge, and executioner at the same time."

John Paul II's relations with the United States have always been complex. Vacillating between gestures of benediction and admonition, on his last U.S. visit in January 1999 the pope told a crowd of the faithful in St. Louis the story of Moses and Pharaoh—with clear allusions to the present day. "As we end the century, and given the radical political changes around the world, America's responsibility to be a model of a truly free, democratic, just, and humane society is increasing," the pontiff declared. "God," he continued, works "in the defense of the earth's lowly and for the liberation of its downtrodden.... God dispels the proud." Power means responsibility and service, not privilege, and the exercise of power is morally justified only when it takes into account the well-being of all.

There is no question but that Karol Wojtyla did everything he could to prevent the war in Iraq—with the same firm resolve he brought to his push for the liberation of Poland at the beginning of his pontificate. Then he was fighting for a liberated Europe, now he was fighting for his vision of global equilibrium and the common responsibility of all peoples to overcome crises, combat threats to peace, and facilitate progress. According to that vision, Europe must serve as one of the pillars in a harmonious structure.

Seldom has the pope become so deeply involved in an issue. And never have his colleagues in the leadership of the Curia resorted to such strong statements. Secretary of state for the Vatican, Cardinal Angelo Sodano, normally a good friend to America, admonished his Washington

FOLLOWING SPREAD

John Paul II's health is visibly worsening. The whole world is witness to his suffering. He now has to pray the annual stations of the cross at the Colosseum in a wheelchair. He often talks about his illness, his suffering, his death. But resigning is unthinkable to him. He is quoted as having said, "Jesus did not climb down from the cross"—then added with a grin, half in jest, half in earnest: "In eternity I will have ample time to rest."

acquaintances during the decisive weeks before the war, asking, "Doesn't what happened in Vietnam tell you anything?" The Vatican's foreign minister, Archbishop Jean-Louis Tauran, stated flatly: "We must choose between the power of right and the right of power. Preventive war is not provided for in the United Nations charter." Even more clearly, the president of the Papal Council for Justice and Freedom, Archbishop Renato Martino, asserted, "We cannot imagine a world policeman acting as a disciplinarian punishing bad behavior."

Small wonder that millions of European Catholics took part in huge demonstrations against the war in mid-February of 2003. In Rome alone some three million people took to the streets. Nuns, priests, religious groups, churchgoers, often people who had never participated in a demonstration before and all of them anything but radical. The *New York Times* reported that the peace demonstrations taking place in Europe were the most impressive of the postwar era. Other American papers suggested that the United States now saw itself confronted with a new superpower—public opinion.

Karol Wojtyla stood in the vanguard of this struggle; he even declared a day of fasting to protest the war, scheduling it for Ash Wednesday. Odd things happened as a result of his appeals. The head of the Anglican Church of England and the Catholic Cardinal of Westminster signed a joint document opposing the military exploit the British prime minister was prepared to embark on. The National Council of Churches (an American organization of non-Catholic Christian denominations with fifty million adherents) called upon the pope to address the United Nations in New York in one more bid for peace.

Despite all of this, the war was unleashed. But global debate about war and peace is by no means ended, as witness the chaotic events in Iraq.

The mystic Karol Wojtyla invoked God's judgment. The prophecy he declared on March 18, the day of Bush's ultimatum to Iraq, has still not ceased to echo: "Anyone who decides that the peaceful means provided by international law are exhausted saddles himself with a heavy responsibility to God, to his conscience, and to history."

IN·HONORE PR POST PA

VRGHESIVS ROMANV

Twenty-five Years of John Paul II

When John Paul II assumed his office on October 16, 1978, Leonid Brezhnev was the Soviet leader, Jimmy Carter the American president, Deng Xiaoping ruler of China, and Helmut Schmidt chancellor of Germany. He has outlasted them all, exceeded their tenures many times over. To the younger generation, the very concept of the pope is synonymous with John Paul II. Wholly immune to the whims of voters or party conventions, and despite physical handicaps, he has kept at his job—unlike bishops, popes are not required to step down at a certain age. His pontificate is currently the third longest in history.

But it is not only the length of his reign that is a near record. John Paul II is the first pope ever to enter the houses of worship of other religions: the synagogue in Rome and the Umayyad mosque in Damascus. Through his personal witness, his charisma, and his gift for drama, John Paul II has unquestionably increased respect for the papacy worldwide. He is a pope for the people, and most especially a pope for peace. In early 2003, in advance of the war in Iraq, he again summoned all his strength—already severely marked by Parkinson's disease—and told ambassadors from around the world at the New Year's reception at the Holy See: "War is never inevitable. It is always a defeat for mankind."

No matter how one evaluates these twenty-five years, John Paul II's successor will have difficulty getting out from under the shadow of this pontificate, which has been a record-breaker in many respects.

PREVIOUS AND FOLLOWING PAGES

The papal jubilee (pp. 190–99). Journalists, photographers, and camera teams take up their positions (pp. 192–93).

Cardinals and the congratulation line (pp. 195–97). Dignitaries from around the world assemble in Rome for the jubilee of the pope's accession.

Ceremonial mass (pp. 198–99). More than fifty thousand believers and more than 250 cardinals and bishops gathered in St. Peter's Square on the evening of October 16, 2003. Pope John Paul II began his address with the same words he used after his election twenty-five years prior: "Open, yes tear open, the gates for Christ!"

Chronology

MAY 18, 1920 Karol Józef Wojtyla is born in Wadowice, near Kraków, the second son of Karol Wojtyla and Emilia Kaczorowska.

1942 He secretly takes up the study of theology.

NOVEMBER 1, 1946 Karol Wojtyla is ordained a priest in Kraków. Subsequently he will receive doctoral degrees in Rome and Kraków and in 1954 qualify as a university lecturer in Kraków. In 1956 he is appointed professor of ethics at the Catholic University of Lublin.

SEPTEMBER 28, 1958 At age thirty-eight, Karol Wojtyla is named suffragan in Kraków and thus becomes the youngest member of the Polish episcopate.

JANUARY 13, 1964 He is named archbishop of Kraków.

JUNE 26, 1967 Pope Paul VI designates him a cardinal.

OCTOBER 16, 1978 After the death of John Paul I, Karol Wojtyla is elected as the first non-Italian pope in more than 450 years. The new pontifex John Paul II becomes the 264th successor of the apostle Peter.

JANUARY 25, 1979 The pope undertakes his first trip abroad, to the Dominican Republic, Mexico, and the Bahamas. Numerous travels, to date to more than 130 countries around the world, will become an important feature of his pontificate.

MARCH 4, 1979 His inaugural encyclical *Redemptor Hominis* (*Mankind's Savior*) is presented, in which John Paul II calls for worldwide recognition of human rights, emphasizing religious freedom and freedom of conscience.

JUNE 2–10, 1979 John Paul II travels to his homeland of Poland for the first time as pope. In subsequent years he will support the union Solidarity, founded in 1980 under the leadership of Lech Walesa, and in so doing contribute greatly to the collapse of Communism in Central and Eastern Europe.

NOVEMBER 15–19, 1980 The pope visits Germany for the first time; he will make subsequent visits in 1987 and 1996.

MAY 13, 1981 In an assassination attempt during a general audience on St. Peter's Square, John Paul II is severely wounded.

MAY 28, 1982 John Paul II sets foot on British soil, the first pope to do so since the Anglicans split with Rome 450 years earlier.

APRIL 13, 1986 John Paul II becomes the first head of the Catholic Church to visit a Jewish house of worship, the synagogue in Rome.

OCTOBER 27, 1986 The pope invites representatives of the world religions to Assisi to take part in a common prayer for peace.

JUNE 30, 1988 John Paul II excommunicates the traditionalist archbishop Marcel Lefebvre, who consecrated bishops without authority.

DECEMBER 1, 1989 The pope receives Mikhail Gorbachev at the Vatican, the first such reception of a general secretary of the Communist Party of the Soviet Union.

NOVEMBER 2, 1992 John Paul II rehabilitates the astronomer Galileo Galilei, condemned by the Inquisition in 1632.

MAY 17, 1993 A new "world catechism" is issued for the first time since 1566.

JUNE 15, 1994 Israel and the Vatican take up full diplomatic relations.

MAY 22, 1994 The apostolic letter *Ordinatio sacerdotalis* supports the Catholic Church's rejection of the ordination of women to the priesthood.

JANUARY 21–26, 1998 The pope makes his first trip to Cuba, during which he calls for freedom for the Catholic Church, democracy, and the lifting of the U.S. economic embargo.

OCTOBER 11, 1998 John Paul II canonizes the German-Jewish nun Edith Stein.

NOVEMBER 20, 1999 The Catholic Church in Germany secedes from the system of advising pregnant women in conflict. German bishops are requested to continue advising such women without issuing the consultation certificate required for a legal abortion.

DECEMBER 24, 1999 As a prelude to the Holy Year 2000 the pope ceremonially opens the Sacred Door in St. Peter's Basilica.

MARCH 12, 2000 For the first time in the history of the Catholic Church, a pope pronounces a comprehensive confession of guilt for Christendom's sins and mistakes in the past two thousand years.

MAY 12–13, 2000 The pope makes his third trip to Fatima, the Portuguese place of pilgrimage, where he beatifies two of the shepherd children to whom the Virgin is said to have appeared in 1917. In addition he thanks the mother of God for saving him from the attempted assassination of May 13, 1981. Shortly afterward the Vatican publishes the so-called Third Secret of Fatima with a commentary by the Congregation for the Doctrine of the Faith.

MAY 18, 2000 The pope celebrates his eightieth birthday with three thousand priests from around the world.

JANUARY 6, 2001 The pope closes the Sacred Door of St. Peter's Basilica, thereby bringing to a close the Holy Year 2000.

FEBRUARY 21, 2001 In the largest consistory in Church history, forty-four churchmen are elevated to cardinal, among them Walter Kasper, Johannes Joachim Degenhardt, and Leo Scheffczyk, as well as the president of the German Conference of Bishops, Karl Lehmann.

MAY 4, 2001 John Paul II visits Greece as the first head of the Catholic Church since the schism between the Orthodox and Roman churches in 1054. In Athens the pope apologizes for the crimes of the crusaders in the year 1204.

MAY 6, 2001 In Damascus John Paul II becomes the first pope to visit a mosque, and prays together with Muslims.

JANUARY 24, 2002 At a peace summit with representatives of the world religions in Assisi the pope and representatives of numerous confessions call for a worldwide coalition for peace and understanding following the terrorist attacks of September 11, 2001.

APRIL 23, 2002 At a crisis summit with U.S. cardinals and bishops in Rome, John Paul II makes it clear that pedophile priests have no place in the Catholic Church. In the United States a series of cases of sexual abuse of minors by priests had previously been exposed.

JUNE 5–9, 2003 The pope undertakes his one-hundredth trip abroad, this time to Croatia.

JUNE 28, 2003 In the postsynodal exhortation *Ecclesia in Europa*, John Paul II again demands that in the process of European unification the Continent's biblical, Christian roots not be forgotten.

JULY 31, 2003 With the consent of the pope, the Congregation for the Doctrine of the Faith under the leadership of Cardinal Joseph Ratzinger calls upon the faithful and Catholic politicians to resist same-sex marriage in a document on "living relationships between homosexual persons."

OCTOBER 16, 2003 Cardinals from all over the world congratulate Pope John Paul II on the twenty-fifth anniversary of his election. Leading politicians praise the eighty-three-year-old's efforts as "pope of peace" and "bridge-builder."

Bibliography

Accattoli, Luigi. *Man of the Millennium: John Paul II*. Boston: Pauline Books and Media, 2000.

———. *When a Pope Asks Forgiveness: The Mea Culpa's of John Paul II*. Boston: St. Paul Books and Media, 1998.

Accattoli, Luigi, and Grzegorz Galazka. *Life in the Vatican with John Paul II*. New York: Universe, 1999.

Bernstein, Carl, and Marco Politi. *His Holiness: John Paul II and the History of Our Time*. Reprint, New York: Penguin, 1997.

Malinski, Mieczyslaw. *Pope John Paul II: The Life of Karol Wojtyla*. New York: Crossroad, 1981.

O'Brien, Darcy. *The Hidden Pope: The Untold Story of a Lifelong Friendship That Is Changing the Relationship Between Catholics and Jews: The Personal Journey of John Paul II and Jerzy Kluger*. Emmaus, Penn.: Rodale Press, 1998.

Reese, Thomas J. *Inside the Vatican: The Politics and Organization of the Catholic Church*. Cambridge, Mass.: Harvard University Press, 1998.

Szulc, Tad. *Pope John Paul II: The Biography*. New York: Simon and Schuster, 1996.

Weigel, George. *Witness to Hope: The Biography of Pope John Paul II*. New York: Perennial, 2001.

About the Authors

Luigi Accattoli, born in Racanati, Italy, in 1943, has been writing for the *Corriere della Sera* for twenty-two years as a Vatican expert and reporter on the pope's travels. He has published widely.

Dr. Heinz-Joachim Fischer was born in 1944. In 1974 he became a political editor at the *Frankfurter Allgemeine Zeitung*, and since 1978 he has served as the paper's Italian and Vatican correspondent in Rome. He has received a number of international prizes for his reporting. In addition to his work as a journalist he is a writer of fiction and nonfiction, including *Die Jahre mit Johannes Paul II. Rechenschaft über ein politisches Pontifikat* (1998) and *Die Nachfolge: Von der Zeit zwischen den Päpsten* (1997).

Arthur Hertzberg, born in Galicia (now Ukraine) in 1921, immigrated to the United States with his family when he was five. He is a religious scholar and rabbi, honorary vice president of the Jewish World Congress, a humanities professor at New York University, and professor emeritus from Dartmouth College. Among his numerous publications are *The Fate of Zionism: A Secular Future for Israel and Palestine* (2003), *A Jew in America: My Life and a People's Struggle for Identity* (2002), and *Jewish Polemics* (1992).

Marco Politi, born in Rome in 1947, is an editor at *La Repubblica*, and has served as a Vatican reporter for more than thirty years. In addition he works for European and U.S. television broadcasters and was for six years a correspondent in Moscow. Together with Carl Bernstein, he wrote *His Holiness: John Paul II and the History of Our Time* (1998), among other publications.

Hansjakob Stehle, born in 1927, served from 1955 to 1963 as an editor and first Polish correspondent for the *Frankfurter Allgemeine Zeitung*. From 1967 to 1989 he worked as a correspondent for the Westdeutscher Rundfunk in Vienna and Rome. Since 1964 he has been a contributor to *Die Zeit* for Italy (especially the Vatican) and Eastern Europe. He has written numerous books on contemporary issues, including *Graue Eminenzen–dunkle Existenzen. Geheimgeschichten aus vatikanischen und anderen Hinterhöfen* (1998) and *Geheimdiplomatie im Vatikan: Die Päpste und die Kommunisten* (1993).

Photograph Credits

AGENCE FRANCE PRESS: Gabriel Bouys: 2–3, 159 top, 161, 162, 175, 190–191, 201; Giuglio Broglio: 153 center left; Derrick Ceyrac: 4, 99, 101, 124–125, 127, 133, 134, 135 top, bottom, 136, 137; Paolo Cocco: 49, 198–199, 200, 205; Walter Dhladhla: 153 bottom left; Dominique Faget: 51; Eric Feferberg: 88, 126; Michel Gangne: 140 top, center, bottom, 141 left, 151 center right; Guillaud: 75; Patrick Hertzog: 197 top; Daniel Janin: 98; Gerard Julien: 178; Menahem Kahana: 168–169; Daniel Luna: 123; Arturo Mari/Vatican Pool: 156; Pierre-Philippe Mercou: 203; Marcel Mochet: 58–59; Sven Nackstrand: 159 top; *Osservatore Romano*/EPA/ANSA: 153 top right; M. Persson: 152 center left; Vincenzo Pinto: 196, 197 bottom, 202; Paul J. Richards: 151 top left; Adalberto Roque: 144; Hans Techt/APA: 152 top left; Marco Ugarte: 122, 151 center left; Pedro Ugarte: 8, 141 right; Vatican Pool/EPA/ANSA: 152 center right, 170. AFP Photo: 1, 107 center, 132, 154–155. ANSA/AFP: 87 top. ANSA/EPA/AFP: 152 top right, 153 top left.

AGENTUR FOCUS: *Contact*—David Burnett: 80–81, 83; Gerard Falcon: 62 left; Chuck Fishman: 66, 85, 92; Gianfranco Gorgoni: 69, 70, 73, 117; Dilip Mehta: 104–105, 107 top; Louie Psihoyos: 129; Alon Reininger; 128, 130, 131.
Contrasto—Tommaso Bonaventura: 151 top right, 172–173, 177, 179, 181, 183, 185, 187, 192–193, 195; Roberto Koch: 61; Massimo Stragusa: 42–43, 138, 139.
Magnum—Bruno Barbey: 91, 97; Gilles Peress: Jacket; Dolf Pressig: 62 right; Fred Mayer: 38–39, 40–41, 47; Raghu Rai: 107 bottom, 109; Ferdinando Scianna: 110–111, 112, 113.
Rapho—Thierry Boccon-Gibod: 119, 121; Henrik Saxgren: 145, 146, 147, 148–149.

ASSOCIATED PRESS: 35.

CATHOLIC PRESS PHOTO: 10.

CORBIS: Bettmann: 37, 82; Fabian Cevallos/Sygma: 87 bottom; Najlah Feanny/SABA: 142–143; Gianni Giansanti: 44.

KNA-BILD: 13 left, 27.

OSSERVATORE ROMANO: Arturo Mari: 46.

SIPA PRESS: Adenis: 151 bottom left; Boccon-Gibod: 63 right, left, 64; Galazka: 151 bottom right, 153 bottom right; Ginies: 153 center right; Laski: 12, 13 right, 15, 16, 19, 20, 24, 31; Marinelli: 152 bottom left; *Osservatore Romano*: 152 bottom right; Setboun: 55, 79; Yaghobzadeh: 165.

Project Manager, English-language edition: Susan Richmond
Editor, English-language edition: Libby Hruska
Jacket Design, English-language edition: Michael Walsh
Design Coordinator, English-language edition: Christine Knorr
Production Coordinator, English-language edition: Kaija Markoe

Library of Congress Cataloging-in-Publication Data

John Paul II : a Pope for the people / essays by Luigi Accattoli ... [et al.] ; translated from the German by Russell Stockman.
p. cm.
Includes bibliographical references and index.
ISBN 0-8109-4984-9 (hardcover)
1. John Paul II, Pope, 1920- 2. Popes—Biography.
I. Accattoli, Luigi.

BX1378.5.J582 2004
282'.092--dc22

2003022921

Printed and bound in Germany
10 9 8 7 6 5 4 3 2 1

Harry N. Abrams, Inc.
100 Fifth Avenue
New York, N.Y. 10011
www.abramsbooks.com

Abrams is a subsidiary of

LA MARTINIÈRE
GROUPE